# Governance, Risk, and Compliance Playbook: A Strategic Guide to Cybersecurity Resilience

Pavan Paidy

# Preface

Organizations need to maintain advanced security measures because cybersecurity threats continue to evolve, so they can follow Governance Risk and Compliance frameworks. The book provides strategic direction to three key organizational groups wanting to increase cybersecurity resilience across a complex digital environment.

Organizations need the combination of Governance, Risk and Compliance to create an effective proactive security system. Appropriate governance design develops rules and responsibility systems while risk management solutions discover threats to eliminate them and compliance serves as a requirement monitoring system. Businesses seeking security strategies need this book, which delivers valuable information about regulatory navigation, risk framework management, and compliance-driven practice implementation.

Organizations need to adjust their security methods because cloud computing has expanded while artificial intelligence has emerged alongside Zero Trust security approaches and new regulatory standards. The book examines current security patterns and delivers implementation advice to corporate security experts who maintain enterprise systems.

This book serves as an inclusive guide which helps professionals develop cybersecurity governance abilities and automate compliance procedures while managing security dangers effectively. The principles in this book have been designed to help organizations build better security resilience while shielding critical assets and sustaining compliance as threats in the environment change constantly.

# Acknowledgments

I would like to express my gratitude to everyone who contributed to the development of this book. Special appreciation goes to my colleagues, mentors, and the cybersecurity community for their invaluable insights and support throughout this journey. Their expertise and feedback have played a crucial role in shaping the content of this book.

I acknowledge the use of grammar tools to refine and enhance the clarity of the writing, ensuring that the technical concepts presented in this book are both precise and accessible. Additionally, MATLAB was utilized to generate several visual representations, aiding in the illustration of complex security models and compliance frameworks.

This book references and integrates several key cybersecurity frameworks, including but not limited to:

- National Institute of Standards and Technology Cybersecurity Framework (NIST CSF)

- General Data Protection Regulation (GDPR)

- Health Insurance Portability and Accountability Act (HIPAA)

- Payment Card Industry Data Security Standard (PCI-DSS)

- Federal Risk and Authorization Management Program (FedRAMP)

- Cloud Computing Compliance Controls Catalog (C5)

- Cloud Security Alliance (CSA) Guidelines

- Zero Trust Architecture (ZTA)

I extend my appreciation to the broader cybersecurity community for their continuous research, innovation, and commitment to strengthening security practices. Their work has provided the foundation for many of the principles discussed in this book.

Finally, I am grateful to my readers for their interest in cybersecurity, risk management, and compliance. It is my hope that this book serves as a valuable resource in navigating the evolving cybersecurity landscape and fostering stronger security resilience across organizations.

# Contents

# III. Compliance :Meeting Regulatory and Industry Standards 135

# 1. Introduction

The essential challenge of cyberspace security affects all types of business organizations across multiple sectors. Digital business operations, alongside the surge of cloud computing and massive data accumulation, have made security vulnerabilities reach their highest point ever. Cybersecurity threats now use complex tactics involving ransomware attacks, social engineering methods, and supply chain exploits. Business fluctuations require organizations to abandon impulsive routines to handle security practices. Businesses must develop an intentional, strategic model that makes Cybre silence the organization's core operation.

Applying Governance Risk Compliance (GRC) standards to modern cyberneticist program development shows its critical position in the introduction section. Organizations that apply GRC framework components through centralized system integration achieve better security standards with regulatory compliance and risk control benefits. The chapter investigates regular organizational implementation obstacles for compliance adoption. It introduces an all-inclusive manual framework that security leaders, compliance officers, and IT professionals can access through this guide.

## 1.1. Overview of Governance, Risk, and Compliance (GRC) in Cybersecurity

Organizations should use Governance Risk Compliance (GRC) as a structured program that unites cybersecurity initiatives with business direction, properly controls security dangers, and fulfils regulatory necessities. GRC enables organizations to build a unified system by uniting security with risk management and compliance tasks, thus ensuring strategic security measures that remain sustainable.

Cybersecurity management within an organization follows established policies and procedures to make decisions through defined structures. Organizations benefit through effective governance by implementing security policies that move from theoretical to active implementation with ongoing monitoring and process improvement. Security control maintenance requires executives to establish their responsibilities, as well as those of the IT teams and compliance officers. Poor governance leads organizations to experience security measures that lack organization, making them respond only after incidents happen with variable standards.

After assessment, risk management processes identify security threats to develop appropriate countermeasures that protect business operations. Organizations must deal with various security perils that generate financial losses through cyber attacks, produce operational interruptions because of security breaches, and inflict reputational destruction when customer data suffers leaks. Businesses can allocate security funding effectively through structured risk management. It enables organizations to identify severe threats and probable risks and prioritize their security investments at the most vulnerable points.

Guidelines from compliance require business operations to fulfil industry-specific regulations, official legal mandates designed for data defence, and security protocols. Several regulatory frameworks, including GDPR and HIPAA PCI,-DSS, and NIST Cybersecurity Framework, require organizations to implement exact security requirements for stopping unauthorized data access and cyber threats. Security standards non-compliance might result in substantial financial penalties, legal sanctions, and damaged customer trust.

Organizations that unite governance with risk management and compliance achieve a defined cybersecurity approach that protects against risks, preserves adherence to regulations, and builds stronger resistance against attacks. A GRC-based strategy allows businesses to take security action before cyber incidents instead of waiting for them to happen.

## 1.2. Importance of an Integrated GRC Approach for Modern Enterprises

Organizations function in a digital environment involving continuous change in cyber threats, intensified business risks, and expanding regulatory requirements. The fragmented governance management, risk, and compliance create security gaps that combine with inefficient policy execution in such environments. Most businesses find managing these three essential security components difficult, so they adopt a defensive security posture instead of taking preventive measures. An integrated Governance Risk and Compliance (GRC) approach develops unified security frameworks that support organizational aims and compliance needs and produce sustainable cyber defenses.

Many companies still handle governance, risk management, and compliance separately. The security departments work on technical controls, but risk management teams follow independent assessments while compliance officers handle regulatory needs with minimal departmental coordination. Security gaps exist along with unnecessary duplicated work while different objectives compete with one another when departments operate independently. Security teams deploy control mechanisms that differ from compliance mandates, and compliance teams concentrate exclusively on audit success without investigating genuine security threats. Implementing an integrated GRC framework distinguishes itself by uniting all security initiatives into a cohesive operation.

Better organization visibility emerges as a primary advantage of uniting GRC frameworks. Security-related issues become evident only after cyber breaches occur in organizations that maintain disorganized strategic frameworks. The coordinated framework of governance risk management compliance enables businesses to actively monitor their security position while detecting threats before exploitation so they can execute concentrated security improvements. Assessing security risks in real-time enables security leaders to make informed choices that merge business targets with regulatory mandates.

The initiative to follow a GRC-based strategy enables organizations to simplify their operations while eliminating performance bottlenecks. Organizations experiencing partitioned governance risk management and compliance activities end up dealing with redundant security measures, duplicated processes throughout their operations, and higher administrative costs. GRC-based strategic alignment makes compliance audits sec, security assessments, and risk management activities support each other without creating unnecessary workload. The integrated model enables businesses to unify their regulatory evaluations because it consolidates their security controls and reporting obligations, ultimately leading to operational simplicity and cost reduction.

Cybersecurity compliance remains challenging mainly because businesses deal with multiple jurisdictions imposing specific regulatory rules. For businesses, compliance functions mainly as paperwork due to their perception that it exists separately from cybersecurity essentials. Trapped in reactive mode, organizations spend excess time rolling out reactive plans instead of designing protective security systems that deliver enduring benefits. Integrating the GRC strategy distributes compliance duties throughout the overall security design instead of managing it independently as periodic evaluations. By establishing ongoing compliance, businesses minimize penalties and legal consequences together with reputational harm which results from non-compliance.

An adequately designed GRC framework supports better interdepartmental cooperation. Organizations must unite security professionals with compliance officers, executive leadership, and end-users and IT teams to address cybersecurity responsibilities because security duty now extends beyond individual departments. The inability of organizations to support teamwork between their departments makes it difficult for them to maintain consistent security policy implementation. Security control deployments by teams usually result in employees not understanding the features, while compliance officers establish difficult-to-enforce requirements alongside executive leaders who lack organizational risk exposure insight. When departments unite through an integrated GRC model, they achieve unified business goals that establish security awareness throughout every organizational activity.

A GRC model with integrated components enables organizations to create security-minded cultural awareness, representing an essential outcome. Security breaches involving human mistakes occur because employees exposed data through phishing schemes and by setting passwords that are easily compromised and poorly handling protected information. Advanced security technologies receive substantial organizational investments, but the human factor is the greatest threat to organizational security. The governance-based method adopts a discipline that focuses on security awareness training and policy implementation across the entire organization structure. A better awareness of cybersecurity core principles and employee understanding of their data security protection responsibilities substantially reduce security incidents.

Educational institutions must stay ahead of the technological curve to prepare for the latest cyber dangers extending past essential security points. Cybercriminals deploy artificial intelligence while adopting advanced attack techniques to bypass corporate security systems, which they operate using automation. Businesses worldwide face three essential security threats: ransomware attacks, supply chain weaknesses and vulnerabilities, and cloud security concerns. Security management without integrated strategy creation hinders business preparations toward modern risks. A GRC framework with proper structure enables businesses to face cyber threats. It helps them monitor new risks through policy adjustments and advanced security deployments for handling developing security issues.

Modern governments and industry regulators strengthen cybersecurity requirements as new standards to defend customer data and infrastructure systems. Businesses not taking proactive actions towards compliance will suffer severe monetary penalties and legal repercussions. The General Data Protection Regulation and the California Consumer Privacy Act demand that organizations to build protective data security measures while ensuring customers understand their data usage practices. Organizations that do not follow these regulations face multiple consequences, including substantial penalties, legal problems, and loss of customer faith. When GRC operates as an integrated practice, it embeds regulatory compliance within security strategies, which enables businesses to fulfill changing legal mandates while enhancing their cybersecurity resistance.

A well-integrated GRC framework emerges prominently

in strategic decision-making activities. The execution of security and risk management decisions mainly stems from compliance checklist approaches instead of collecting real-threat intelligence within the business landscape. Such security strategies require organizations to spend money on controls that fail to protect their top threat areas. Businesses achieve improved budget efficiency for security expenditures by merging governance structures with risk evaluation and compliance oversight activities. Security funding first goes to risk-based decision-making systems' most significant threats since actual dangers matter more than regulatory requirements.

The implementation of GRC principles must extend to external vendors and cloud service providers for organizations that use their services. Third-party systems represent a significant source of cyberattacks since attackers identify security weaknesses in vendor networks to penetrate more extensive enterprise infrastructure. Lacking an integrated system for vendor risk management makes businesses incomprehensible about the security status of their supply chain networks. An extensive GRC framework enables organizations to evaluate their vendors' security hazards while compelling adherence to security terms and validating that external entities maintain equal standards with internal personnel.

Complete GRC integration proves essential because organizations that choose not to adopt such a strategy face growing obstacles while achieving security and compliance goals. Organizations experience severe consequences from fragmenting their security approach because they face elevated operational dangers, compliance breakdowns, and heightened susceptibility to security breaches. Security readiness against emerging threats becomes stronger for companies that merge governance with risk management and compliance systems for their security framework while reducing legal risks and building sustainable security models according to long-term business goals.

By adopting an organized GRC method, businesses strengthen their cybersecurity resistance and build foundations for future business development. Businesses that uphold excellent standards of security governance and regulatory compliance secure an upper hand through customer and investor trust and partner willingness to work with them. Organizations that adopt GRC principles determine compliance and security obligations and function as competitive success tools in business operations.

Organizations achieve successful business continuation through daily operations by integrating security governance, risk management, and compliance practices to develop a security-focused company environment that protects customer information and encourages innovative approaches. Organizations can work confidently in a complex digital environment after implementing an adequately structured GRC framework that protects them against cyber risks.

# 1.3. Key Challenges Organizations Face in Meeting Compliance Standards

The vital function of compliance in cybersecurity remains difficult for organizations because they face complications when attempting to fulfill regulatory mandates. The extensive number of cybersecurity regulations, fast-paced technological developments, and changing cyber threats define an overwhelming and complex regulatory environment. Businesses need to understand compliance frameworks while implementing them in their operations but should also develop evolving security policies that address new security risks. Organizations that fail to maintain compliance standards will face legal penalties which combine with damage to their reputation and heavy monetary penalties. The security objectives behind compliance initiatives prove challenging to most businesses when they try to connect compliance standards to their actual business activities.

Organizations face their biggest hurdle because compliance frameworks have very complicated regulations. Organizations doing business in multiple regions must follow unique regulatory requirements with separate reporting protocols and specific mandate regulations. Businesses must fulfill separate provisions under the General Data Protection Regulation, the Health Insurance Portability and Accountability Act, the Payment Card Industry Data Security Standard, and the Cybersecurity Maturity Model Certification. The security principles among regulations might overlap, but their implementation rules differ, which creates challenges for businesses to create a single compliance approach. Several businesses encounter difficulties because they face regulatory duplications sec,urity control mismatches, and extensive audit-related responsibilities.

Multinational corporations face even more extensive complexity when it comes to compliance demands. A business dealing with operations in the United States, European Union, and Asia must simultaneously fulfill different requirements from multiple compliance frameworks. This process demands organizations to spend time and resources tracking different security requirements for interpretation and implementation. Non-compliance penalties issued by regulators constitute a significant risk for companies that do not update their policies. These penalties include financial fines and operational limitations.

Businesses of all sizes especially face significant challenges regarding compliance expenses. The process of compliance forces organizations to deploy security controls while doing risk assessments, implementing audits, and maintaining extensive documentation through such steps which require primary financial resources. Despite having compliance teams and cybersecurity budgets, large companies face challenges because small businesses frequently avoid budgeting enough funds for necessary compliance projects. Organizations bear double financial costs for compliance activities because they must develop security measures, funding staff training, and policy-making and compliance surveillance.

Organizations face additional challenges in compliance initiatives because of the shortage of qualified cybersecurity experts and financial budget deficits. Security compliance depends on competent employees who deploy security frameworks and perform risk evaluation and audit responsibilities. A worldwide shortage of trained cybersecurity experts emerged when the occupation demand surged higher than the number of available experts could address. The challenge for companies remains high because they struggle to find experienced personnel in compliance officer roles, security analyst positions, and risk management specialist functions. Insufficient cybersecurity expertise exposes companies to compliance risks because their limited security personnel struggle to track security policy execution and changes in legal requirements.

Third-party risk management leads to substantial compliance difficulties for various organizations. Many firms now execute essential business operations through partnerships with external vendors, cloud service providers, and supply chain partners. Safety threats offset the advantages of outsourcing it creates. Supply chain vulnerabilities occur because third-party vendors fail to adopt the same compliance standards their organization clients must follow. Because of weak security practices in their systems, cybercriminals achieve unauthorized access to sensitive data at third-party locations. Organizations need their vendors to follow security regulations, yet many struggle to understand how well their third-party vendors follow security requirements. Lack of oversight in the extended supply network hampers risk evaluation and enforces compliance standards throughout the enterprise system.

Third-party compliance becomes more complicated to

manage due to cloud computing environments. The number of businesses moving toward cloud environments makes it progressively troublesome to maintain compliance within hybrid cloud environments. Under shared responsibility models cloud service providers mandate security split into two sectors: their and customer's commitments. Multiple organizations experience difficulty determining their particular compliance duties about these regulatory frameworks. Without defined ownership, there is a higher likelihood of security gaps, potential breaches, and configuration errors compliance failures. A lack of established cloud security compliance strategy exposes organizations to non-compliance with all data privacy, encryption, and access control standards.

Real-life cybersecurity threats do not align with existing compliance standards, which present a critical problem for organizations. The continuously evolving threat environment surpasses the established baseline standards which regulatory frameworks present as security requirements. Cybercriminals actively produce advanced attack procedures consisting of artificial intelligence-controlled threats, supply chain vulnerabilities, and zero-day attacks. Even though organizations achieve technical compliance through checklists, they remain at risk because these guidelines might fail to cover emerging security threats. Businesses which rely exclusively on regulatory requirements to build their security approach operate at risk of inadequate protection against complex cyber threats. Security implementation within operational culture receives minimal attention from certain organizations focusing only on audit compliance. This method known as "check-the-box" compliance lets organizations fulfill basic legal obligations but fails to enhance their actual security position. Companies deploy security controls during audits but drop those security protocols after audits are complete. This temporary security approach increases short- and long-term security vulnerabilities, resulting in continued non-compliance issues.

Security operations become more efficient when organizations move to real-time monitoring and enhancement of compliance status through continuous monitoring instead of limited audit assessments. The integrated workflow of continuous compliance enables security automation for real-time risk monitoring, which enforces policies through proactive measures to sustain compliance against shifting security threats. Organizations using automated compliance solutions gain better tracking of regulatory updates and security analysis, which creates automatic audit documentation for security personnel. Organizations that make compliance part of their regular business procedures will reduce risks while better detecting upcoming security threats.

Organizations face challenges in their compliance efforts because resistance to cultural changes exists within their operations. Most workers treat compliance demands as unnecessary bureaucracy instead of security requirements. Staff members who lack training and awareness programs tend to break security policies, which results in unintentional non-compliance issues. Achieving compliance success requires organizations to develop a security culture that makes all employees understand their responsibility for sensitive information protection. Organizations must devote ongoing resources for employee training while developing engagement programs and leadership backing to strengthen security best practice understanding among staff members.

Businesses need to anticipate the rising impact of artificial intelligence and machine learning techniques that will protect systems from cyberattacks and supervise compliance situations. The enhanced threat detection abilities provided by AI security solutions generate new compliance problems along with their benefits. Security operations using AI face new regulatory requirements from governments and industry regulators because organizations must demonstrate transparency while maintaining fairness and accountability in their decision-making systems that employ artificial intelligence. Business entities without AI compliance elements in their security plans risk future legal inspections by regulatory bodies.

Organizations require dynamic compliance strategies to address modern, sophisticated threats and growing regulatory requirements. They need to view compliance obligations as a security-enhancing advantage that builds customer trust and strengthens their protection against cyber threats. Organizations that build compliance integration throughout their security framework will reduce security risks. This success spans from their investment in experienced personnel to their deployment of automated systems.

Businesses at every scale will face compliance standards as a persistent organizational challenge. Organizations implementing structured ongoing compliance approaches achieve regulatory compliance and strengthen their digital security culture to defend assets against persistent threats.

# 1.4. How This Book Helps Security Leaders, Compliance Officers, and IT Professionals

As such, this book is intended to be a go-to guide for security leaders and compliance officers, IT administrators, and others responsible for securing corporate assets in a fast-changing world. As cyberattacks continue to increase, regulatory complexities abound, and threats grow more sophisticated, professionals in security must embrace a structured, proactive approach to governance, risk management, and compliance. It offers a gradual approach to implementing a successful security framework, ensuring that cybersecurity goals are in lock step with business targets, and that organizations are able to successfully traverse the regulatory landscape without fear.

Systematic cybersecurity is hardly simple, but security leaders have to balance multiple priorities, and their challenges are constant, from preventing cyber incidents and critical infrastructure attacks to ensuring compliance with regulations and third-party risk management. Lack of consistency in security practices often leads to fragmented security approaches, which are a goldmine for cybercriminals. This book guides readers in establishing a common governance framework for enabling cybersecurity resilience, risk-based decision-making across the enterprise, and securing every business process.

Chief Information Security Officers and IT managers will find detailed guidance on developing governance structures that align security efforts with broader business objectives. Cybersecurity is no longer just an IT concern but a fundamental component of corporate strategy. Organizations need clear policies, defined roles, and robust security frameworks to manage risks effectively. This book explores best practices from leading cybersecurity frameworks, such as the National Institute of Standards and Technology Cybersecurity Framework and the International Organization for Standardization 27001 standard. It offers practical insights into how organizations can implement these standards in real-world environments, ensuring that security policies remain adaptable to evolving threats.

Managers within IT departments will enhance their capability to execute risk management strategies which prioritize security investments depending on their potential influence. Organizational resource deployment faces challenges following compliance requirements without focusing on the critical threats. The book offers methods to evaluate cyber threats while spotting essential weaknesses, and then puts forth protection measures that generate quantifiable results to strengthen organizational resistance to attacks. The security guidelines in this work focus on protecting contemporary IT systems as organizations become more dependent on cloud solutions, external providers, and distributed work arrangements.

The duties of compliance officers consist of monitoring organizations for adherence to legal mandates and regulatory standards. Organizations generally handle compliance work as minor administrative duties instead of establishing it within their strategic security framework. The book covers four significant regulations, the General Data Protection Regulation,

Health Insurance Portability and Accountability Act, Payment Card Industry Data Security Standard, and additional rules tailored for specific industries. Readers can understand regulatory requirement interpretation methods and strategies to synchronize security measures with legal mandates and automate operations to cut compliance tasks and improve reporting efficiency through this text.

Organizations dealing with regulatory audits face significant difficulties, especially when they operate across multiple jurisdictions that generate duplicative compliance obligations. Implementing security regulations causes compliance teams to face difficulties with documentation management, inconsistent reporting, and complex security regulation compliance demonstration. This book presents operational methodologies to prepare for audits,form internal security assessments, and maintain an ongoing compliance posture instead of treating it as an annual or quarterly process. Organizations that embrace proactive compliance prevent audit-related stress at the last minute while protecting themselves from non-compliance fines and building lasting trust with regulatory bodies and their stakeholders.

Professional risk managers need an extensive presentation of the methods used to find cyber risks alongside their evaluation and defense procedures. The absence of formal risk management structures enables security gaps throughout organizations, leading to harm in their financial resources and operational and reputational areas. The book explains thorough risk evaluation frameworks combining qualitative and quantitative technique assessments, scenario-based risk modeling, and security metrics for ongoing risk tracking.

The evaluation of contemporary security threats, including ransomware sup,ply chain attacks, and insider threats, becomes possible for readers through this content. This enables security programs to stay agile and aligned with future needs.

Effective risk management becomes clearest when real-life organizational scenarios are observed. The book investigates crucial security violations and regulatory compliance instances by studying their failure points, exposing exploitation mechanisms, and identifying organizational defenses that could have limited the impact. Real business situations demonstrated through case studies give security professionals essential lessons, which lead them to prevent recurring mistakes while adopting established security tactics from the field.

Organization security professionals must overcome the increased complexity of cybersecurity systems that are becoming prominent in their operations. Cutting-edge security teams face the obstacle of defending their networks because employees work remotely, depend on cloud infrastructure, and have expanding supply chain connections that require modern defense strategies. The book outlines how to deploy Zero Trust security models, teaches cloud workloads security methods, and provides step-by-step guidance to build robust access management structures. Professionals who understand how to implement security principles across different platforms will safeguard their organizations from established and future cyber risks.

This book contains step-by-step insights that working professionals can apply immediately. It outlines fundamental concepts and explains their meaning, delivering comprehensive guidance for accomplishing each task. The book offers templates, best practices, and checklists to simplify security management steps, enabling easier cyber integration in workplace operations.

This book teaches readers what they need to build governance risk management and compliance strategies that perform steadfastly. Security leaders gain the necessary framework to construct security governance structures that link to business executive priorities. Compliance officers will better understand regulatory control deployment methods that preserve business flexibility. The IT managers in this book will receive guidance on creating security programs that reduce business risks through an operational efficiency structure.

This publication is a beneficial reference guide for everyone at different cybersecurity and risk management stages. The information in this book will benefit the entire organization, whether it wants to establish new security programs or improve existing ones.

# Part I.

# Governance – Establishing a Strong Cybersecurity Framework

# 2. Understanding Governance in Cybersecurity

This chapter will focus on the key players in governance, including security and IT leaders, risk committees, and compliance teams. Each of these groups contributes to the development of the governance framework. We will outline transparent steps organizations can take to establish effective cybersecurity governance that aligns with their daily operations and legal requirements and addresses emerging threats.

Real-world examples will illustrate the consequences of poor governance, underscoring the importance of clear rules, accountability, and an improvement plan. This chapter aims to help create a structure that enhances security, boosts resilience, complies with regulations, and better manages risks.

## 2.1. Definition and Role of Governance in Cybersecurity

Cybersecurity governance is the structured approach that organizations implement to manage security risks, establish oversight, and ensure compliance with regulatory and industry standards. In an era where digital transformation is reshaping business operations, cybersecurity has evolved beyond a technical function into a fundamental component of corporate governance. Organizations that fail to establish governance frameworks often struggle with fragmented security efforts, inconsistent policy enforcement, and weak regulatory adherence, leaving them vulnerable to cyber threats.

The primary purpose of cybersecurity governance is to define the roles, responsibilities, and decision-making structures necessary to manage security effectively. Governance ensures that security policies align with business objectives, providing a framework for executive leadership, risk management teams, and compliance officers to work collaboratively in protecting an organization's digital assets. Security initiatives can become reactive and disjointed without governance, leading to a lack of accountability, inadequate risk mitigation, and compliance failures. A structured governance model fosters a proactive security culture where security risks are identified, assessed, and managed systematically.

Organizations adopt governance frameworks based on globally recognized security standards to create a structured approach to cybersecurity. Established frameworks such as the National Institute of Standards and Technology Cybersecurity Framework, the International Organization for Standardization standard for information security management systems, and the Control Objectives for Information and Related Technologies framework provide structured methodologies for implementing security governance. These frameworks help organizations define risk tolerance levels, establish security policies, and implement technical and administrative controls to mitigate cybersecurity threats.

One of the fundamental components of governance in cybersecurity is developing and enforcing security policies. These policies are the foundation of an organization's security posture, outlining the rules and guidelines for data protection, access control, identity and access management, third-party risk management, and incident response procedures. A well-governed cybersecurity program ensures that these policies are documented and integrated into daily business operations through clear communication, employee training, and policy enforcement mechanisms.

Risk management is essential to cybersecurity governance, providing a structured approach to identifying, evaluating, and mitigating security risks. Organizations operate in an environment where ransomware attacks, phishing campaigns, zero-day vulnerabilities, and supply chain compromises continue to evolve. Governance frameworks enable organizations to implement risk assessment methodologies that quantify security risks and prioritize mitigation efforts. The Factor Analysis of Information Risk model is one such approach that allows organizations to quantify cybersecurity risks in financial terms, making it easier for executive leadership to understand the impact of security threats. Similarly, the National Institute of Standards and Technology Risk Management Framework and the International Organization for Standardization standard for risk management provide structured methodologies for assessing and mitigating security threats.

Governance also plays a crucial role in ensuring risk management is an ongoing process rather than a one-time assessment. Cyber threats are dynamic, and organizations must continuously update their risk management strategies based on emerging threats, security analytics, and real-time monitoring data. A well-defined governance model ensures that security leaders integrate risk assessments into daily security operations, leveraging intelligence from security information and event management systems, threat intelligence platforms, and security analytics tools. Governance-driven risk management also involves monitoring security risks across cloud environments, third-party vendors, and interconnected supply chain networks, ensuring that security controls extend beyond traditional on-premises infrastructure.

A significant aspect of cybersecurity governance is ensuring regulatory and industry standards compliance. Governments and industry regulators have established strict cybersecurity mandates to protect sensitive data and critical infrastructure. Organizations that handle customer data, financial transactions, or healthcare information must comply with the General Data Protection Regulation, the California Consumer Privacy Act, the Health Insurance Portability and Accountability Act, and the Payment Card Industry Data Security Standard. Failure to comply with these regulations can result in financial penalties, legal liabilities, and reputational damage.

Effective governance ensures that security policies align with compliance obligations, integrating regulatory requirements into security operations rather than treating compliance as a separate function. A governance-driven compliance model involves conducting regular security audits, maintaining up-to-date security documentation, and implementing security controls that align with regulatory expectations. Organizations that adopt a continuous compliance model rather than a periodic compliance checklist approach are better positioned to navigate evolving regulatory landscapes and avoid last-minute compliance gaps.

Beyond regulatory compliance, governance frameworks support cybersecurity certifications, demonstrating an organization's commitment to security best practices. Certifications such as the International Organization for Standardization certification for information security management, the System and Organization Controls 2 framework, and the Federal Risk and Authorization Management Program establish security credibility for businesses operating in regulated industries. Governance ensures that security policies remain aligned with certification requirements, reducing the risk of compliance failures and audit deficiencies.

The role of executive leadership in cybersecurity governance is essential in ensuring that security initiatives receive the necessary resources, funding, and strategic support. Cybersecurity governance must be considered a board-level priority, with executive leadership actively participating in security decision-making processes. Organizations that struggle to secure budgets for cybersecurity initiatives often face challenges articulating the business impact of security risks. A governance-driven approach addresses this challenge by incorporating risk quantification, key indicators, and financial impact assessments into security reporting. By presenting cybersecurity risks in business terms, security teams can improve executive buy-in and ensure that security investments align with business risk management strategies.

Another critical function of governance is the development of security awareness and training programs. Human error remains one of the leading causes of security breaches, and governance frameworks ensure that employees at all levels receive security training tailored to their roles. Governance ensures that organizations implement structured training programs that educate employees on recognizing phishing attempts, preventing social engineering attacks, and adhering to secure data handling practices. Security awareness programs must extend beyond employee training to include executive leadership, third-party vendors, and contractors with access to organizational networks.

Despite its significance, many organizations face challenges in establishing effective cybersecurity governance models. One of the most common obstacles is organizational resistance to change, where employees and leadership may be reluctant to adopt new security policies or governance measures that introduce stricter compliance requirements. Governance frameworks must include clear communication strategies that emphasize the importance of security policies and demonstrate how governance supports overall business continuity. Another challenge is the fragmentation of security governance across hybrid IT environments, particularly with the widespread adoption of cloud computing and remote work models. Governance must extend beyond traditional security perimeters to cover cloud governance, multi-cloud risk management, and endpoint security policies.

A well-implemented governance model ensures that organizations periodically evaluate their security policies, risk management frameworks, and compliance programs. Continuous security assessments, internal security audits, and governance reviews help organizations maintain an adaptive security posture that evolves with emerging threats. Security governance must also integrate performance measurement metrics, including incident response effectiveness, compliance adherence, and security maturity levels. Organizations prioritizing governance as a strategic function are better equipped to mitigate cybersecurity risks, maintain regulatory compliance, and build long-term resilience against cyber threats.

Cybersecurity governance is foundational to an organization's security strategy, integrating risk management, compliance, and executive oversight into a structured framework. It ensures that security initiatives are aligned with business goals, regulatory requirements, and industry best practices, providing a proactive approach to security management. Organizations that establish strong governance frameworks benefit from improved security resilience, better regulatory preparedness, and greater executive-level engagement in cybersecurity initiatives. By embedding governance into daily operations, businesses can create a security-first culture that supports long-term cybersecurity success.

## 2.2. Key Stakeholders in Cybersecurity Governance

Cybersecurity governance is a structured approach to managing security risks, ensuring regulatory compliance, and aligning security initiatives with business objectives. It is not a responsibility that falls on a single team or department but a collective effort involving multiple stakeholders across an organization. Without clear governance structures, cybersecurity programs can become fragmented, leading to inefficiencies, misalignment with business goals, and increased exposure to cyber threats.

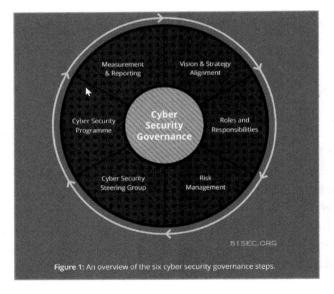

Figure 1: An overview of the six cyber security governance steps.

Figure 2.1.: An overview of the six key cybersecurity governance components.

Effective cybersecurity governance comprises six fundamental components: vision and strategy alignment, roles and responsibilities, risk management, cybersecurity steering groups, cybersecurity programs, and measurement and reporting. These components provide a structured framework that allows organizations to establish clear policies, define security responsibilities, and continuously evaluate the effectiveness of their cybersecurity efforts. When all these components work together, they create a resilient cybersecurity environment that supports long-term business growth while mitigating security risks.

Cybersecurity governance is rooted in aligning vision and strategy with business goals. Security is not separate but an integral part of an organization's overall strategy. Executive leaders such as the Chief Information Security and Chief Information Officer are key in bridging the gap between security goals and business drivers, operational efficiency, and regulatory compliance. A robust governance framework provides assurance that security investments are prioritized based on risk assessments that align with the organization's mission.

The dispensation of roles and responsibilities is one of the most essential facets of governance. The Chief Information Security Officer oversees the organization's security posture, policies, and threat response. The CIO embeds security in tech operations, infrastructure management, and digital transformation. Risk committees oversee the management of cybersecurity risk. At the same time, compliance teams help ensure adherence to industry regulations such as the General Data Protection Regulation and the Health Insurance Portability and Accountability Act. Clearly defining roles and responsibilities enhances visibility, facilitates collaboration, and improves security decision-making.

Risk management is one of the key aspects of cyber-security governance, allowing organizations to identify, assess, and mitigate security risks in an orderly manner. Organizations are increasingly adopting a proactive approach to risk assessment to stay ahead of evolving threats. Risk management committees evaluate potential risks, assess the impact of security breaches, and guide mitigation efforts. Integrating risk management into governance processes ensures that organizations focus on addressing critical vulnerabilities based on threat intelligence rather than applying generic security controls that may not be effective.

A cybersecurity steering group plays a vital role in governance by ensuring security efforts are well-coordinated across different departments. This group includes security, IT, compliance, legal, and executive leadership representatives who work together to align security policies with business objectives. Their primary responsibilities involve evaluating security programs, offering strategic guidance, and ensuring consistent policy enforcement. Organizations that establish such groups gain better decision-making processes, improved risk assessments, and a more structured approach to cybersecurity governance.

A firmly structured cybersecurity program ensures that security policies are effectively implemented and seamlessly integrated into daily business operations. These programs include initiatives such as security awareness training, incident response planning, access control measures, and vendor risk management.

Organizations encourage employees, IT teams, and compliance officers to protect sensitive information by fostering a security-conscious work culture. Additionally, security programs incorporate third-party security assessments to evaluate the security stance of vendors, cloud service providers, and external partners.

Measurement and reporting are key components of cybersecurity governance, helping organizations analyze the effectiveness of their security policies. Establishing security metrics and key performance indicators (KPIs) enables teams to track the impact of security initiatives. Compliance teams perform internal audits to ensure regulatory compliance, while security analysts leverage monitoring tools and incident reports to identify vulnerabilities and assess risks. Furthermore, measurement and reporting are crucial in communicating security risks to executives, ensuring well-justified security investments and efficient resource allocation.

When all six components of cybersecurity governance work seamlessly together, organizations can develop a structured and effective security strategy. However, challenges often emerge when security teams work in isolation or when executive leadership fails to integrate cybersecurity into broader business decisions. To address these issues, companies should promote cross-functional collaboration, encourage open communication between security and IT teams, and continuously refine their governance frameworks to keep up with evolving threats.

Beyond protecting systems and data, strong cybersecurity governance also enhances a company's reputation and customer trust. Businesses that establish robust security policies and governance frameworks send a clear message: they take data protection and regulatory compliance seriously. With growing concerns over how companies handle sensitive information, having a transparent, well-structured governance approach reassures customers, investors, and regulators that security is a top priority. This is especially critical in finance, healthcare, and e-commerce, where a data breach can lead to severe financial and reputational damage.

Looking ahead, cybersecurity governance will continue to evolve as technology advances and cyber threats become more complex. Tools like AI-powered security analytics, automated compliance monitoring, and real-time threat intelligence platforms are transforming how organizations detect, prevent, and respond to risks. To stay ahead, businesses must constantly update their security strategies, invest in cybersecurity training, and implement policies that balance security, compliance, and business innovation.

Ultimately, cybersecurity governance isn't a one-time project—it's an ongoing process that requires constant assessment and adaptation. Organizations that align security with business goals, define clear security roles, implement strong risk management strategies, and foster collaboration through cybersecurity steering groups are better equipped to handle today's rapidly changing threat landscape. By integrating these governance components into their core business strategy, companies can build a resilient security framework that mitigates cyber threats and supports long-term growth and regulatory compliance.

# 2.3. Case Study: Governance Failures and Their Consequences

The 2017 Equifax data breach remains one of history's most significant cybersecurity failures, affecting nearly 147.9 million individuals in the United States and 8,000 in Canada. The breach exposed sensitive personal and financial data and highlighted severe governance, risk management, and cybersecurity oversight deficiencies. Weak governance structures, lack of accountability, and failure to enforce security policies all contributed to an incident that could have been prevented. Examining this breach provides valuable insights into how cybersecurity governance failures can lead to catastrophic consequences.

Figure 2.2.: Timeline and impact of the 2017 Equifax data breach.

The Equifax breach began on May 13, 2017, when attackers exploited a known vulnerability in the Apache Struts web application framework used in Equifax's dispute resolution portal. This vulnerability was publicly disclosed in March 2017, and security patches were made available, yet Equifax failed to apply these updates promptly. Fulfilling security patch management policies was one of this case's most critical governance lapses. The breach was discovered on July 29, more than two months after the initial compromise, but Equifax delayed public disclosure until September 7, raising concerns about transparency and incident response governance.

As shown in Figure 2.2, the breach had a massive impact, affecting nearly 44 percent of the U.S. population. The data stolen included 209,000 credit card numbers, 182,000 dispute resolution documents, Social Security numbers, birth dates, home addresses, and driver's license numbers. The delayed response and inadequate security monitoring contributed to prolonged exposure, allowing attackers to extract sensitive information over an extended period.

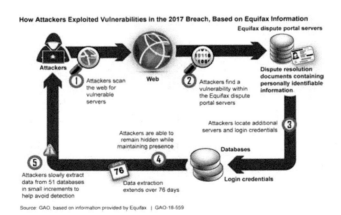

Figure 2.3.: How attackers exploited vulnerabilities in the 2017 Equifax breach.

A deeper analysis of the attack process, as illustrated in Figure 2.3, reveals how governance failures allowed attackers to remain undetected for an extended period. The attackers followed a structured attack methodology, beginning with scanning the internet for vulnerable servers. Once they identified the Equifax dispute portal's weakness, they exploited the Apache Struts vulnerability to gain initial access. They then proceeded to locate additional servers and steal login credentials, which enabled them to expand their foothold within the Equifax network.

One of the most alarming aspects of this breach was the prolonged presence of attackers within Equifax's systems. For 76 days, attackers systematically extracted data from 51 databases in small increments to evade detection. This extended data exfiltration period indicates critical weaknesses in Equifax's security governance, particularly in security monitoring, intrusion detection, and threat response capabilities. Strong governance frameworks emphasize continuous security monitoring and proactive threat detection, which could have mitigated the scale of this breach. The lack of real-time tracking allowed attackers to extract sensitive customer data without triggering immediate alerts.

The Equifax case also exposed major governance failures related to incident response and regulatory compliance. Companies handling sensitive customer information must have clear protocols for detecting, containing, and reporting security incidents. In this case, governance failures led to detection and public disclosure delays, undermining consumer confidence and increasing regulatory scrutiny. Organizations with well-structured cybersecurity governance frameworks have predefined incident response procedures that ensure timely action, rapid containment, and clear communication with stakeholders.

The financial impact of the breach was enormous. Equifax faced legal penalties and regulatory fines exceeding 700 million dollars. The breach led to increased regulatory oversight and stricter compliance requirements, reinforcing the importance of strong security governance in preventing future incidents. The reputational damage was equally severe, as consumers lost trust in Equifax's ability to safeguard their personal information. Governance failures caused immediate financial repercussions and long-term effects on brand reputation and customer confidence.

This breach powerfully reminds us of the critical role governance plays in cybersecurity. Organizations must enforce security policies at all levels, with clear accountability for risk management, vulnerability patching, and incident response. Governance structures should mandate routine security audits, penetration testing, and proactive threat monitoring to detect vulnerabilities before they can be exploited. A well-governed security framework integrates regulatory compliance with cybersecurity best practices, ensuring that organizations meet legal obligations while proactively defending against cyber threats.

The Equifax case underscores the importance of adopting a proactive governance approach that prioritizes risk assessment, security monitoring, and regulatory compliance. Strong governance frameworks empower security teams with the authority and resources to enforce policies, mitigate risks, and respond effectively to incidents. The failure to prioritize cybersecurity governance exposes organizations to regulatory penalties and erodes customer trust and business credibility.

As cyber threats evolve, organizations must continuously refine their cybersecurity governance models. Integrating artificial intelligence-driven threat detection, real-time monitoring systems, and automated compliance reporting can enhance governance capabilities and minimize the risk of breaches. Equifax's lessons should serve as a blueprint for other organizations, emphasizing that cybersecurity governance is not optional but an essential component of a resilient security strategy.

The Equifax data breach highlights the devastating consequences of cybersecurity governance failures. From poor patch management to inadequate security monitoring and delayed incident response, multiple governance breakdowns contributed to the breach's severity. By enforcing stricter governance policies, improving security oversight, and adopting advanced threat detection mechanisms, organizations can strengthen their cybersecurity resilience and prevent similar breaches in the future.

## 2.4. Q&A Section

Q: What is the role of cybersecurity governance?

A: It ensures security policies, risk management, and compliance align with business goals.

Q: How does governance differ from management?

A: Governance sets policies and oversight; management handles execution.

Q: Why is stakeholder collaboration important?

A: It prevents security gaps and aligns risk management with business needs.

Q: What are the risks of weak governance?

A: It leads to breaches, penalties, poor oversight, and compliance failures.

Q: How can organizations improve governance?

A: Define roles, conduct audits, and use security frameworks like NIST and ISO.

Q: What role does compliance play in governance?

A: It ensures legal and industry standards are met to avoid penalties.

Q: How can governance support business innovation?

A: Risk-based policies enable secure innovation without slowing progress.

Q: What lessons come from failures like Equifax?

A: Delayed patching, weak monitoring, and poor governance worsen breaches.

Q: How should governance adapt to new threats?

A: Regular updates, AI-driven threat detection, and proactive strategies.

Q: What is the future of cybersecurity governance?

A: AI, automation, zero-trust, and global compliance will shape governance.

# 3. Frameworks and Standards for Cybersecurity Governance

Implementing cybersecurity governance frameworks helps organizations organize their security risk management activities and establish regulatory compliance standards and security policy definitions. Organizations must implement governance models that protect security interests by following business strategy objectives. Organizations use many international and industry-specific frameworks that help them define security measures and stay compliant while minimizing security risks.

This chapter examines three major security governance frameworks, beginning with the International Organization for Standardization 27001 standard, then moving to the National Institute of Standards and Technology Cybersecurity Framework, and ending with the Center for Internet Security Controls. Frameworks must be selected following assessments of industry requirements, organizational risk exposure, and operational requirements. The discussion emphasizes establishing governance strategies that reflect business objectives to make cybersecurity initiatives support organizational achievement.

# 3.1. Overview of Leading Security Frameworks: ISO 27001, NIST CSF, CIS Controls

Organizations use structured cybersecurity frameworks to handle their risk challenges while defending their data and following the requirements of their regulatory standards. They must use security frameworks that match their operational specifications, risk capacity, and regulatory requirements. A correctly selected framework serves as the base that enables businesses to deploy security policies, handle cyber risks, and advance their constant security practice.

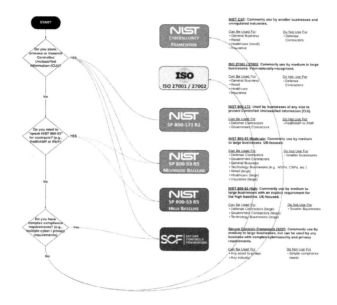

Figure 3.1.: Decision tree for selecting cybersecurity
governance frameworks.

Different cybersecurity frameworks require selection
based on organizational handling of controlled unclassified information, contracts, and specific industry regulations. Figure 3.1 illustrates a structured
approach to selecting cybersecurity frameworks based
on these considerations. Numerous organizations implement three primary framework systems: the International Organization for Standardization 27001
standard, the National Institute of Standards and
Technology Cybersecurity Framework, and the Center for Internet Security Controls.

The globally recognized information security management system framework 27001 standard exists under
the International Organization for Standardization.

Organizations can handle and reduce information security threats through its standardized approach, protecting the confidentiality and integrity of available sensitive data. The standardized framework delivers global applicability in protection requirements within finance sectors such as healthcare organizations and government entities. According to the 27001 standards of the International Organization for Standardization, organizations must create risk management systems, then deploy security controls, and keep tracking the performance of their security measures. Multiple companies choose to achieve certification through this framework as it shows their status of following global data security requirements.

The National Institute of Standards and Technology Cybersecurity Framework is a customizable risk-based security platform that supports organizations to handle and minimize their cybersecurity threats. The National Institute of Standards and Technology developed this framework in the United States, and various organizations from the public and private sectors apply its usage. The National Institute of Standards and Technology framework serves organizations better than the International Organization for Standardization 27001 standard because it enables custom implementation of best practices that map organization-specific security requirements. The framework's core functions include identifying, protecting, detecting, responding, and recovering. The functions allow organizations to build security strategies that connect business targets while sustaining cyber threat resistance.

The twenty security controls within the Center for Internet Security Controls serve as a prioritized framework that enables organizations to fight against typical cyber threats. The security controls organized by the Center for Internet Security include secure configuration management, continuous vulnerability assessment identity and access management, and incident response planning. Organizations that require an active security governance model should find the framework beneficial because of its tactical approach. Small and medium-sized enterprises choose the Center for Internet Security Controls because it enables secure cybersecurity operations through defined procedures instead of requiring strict compliance regulations.

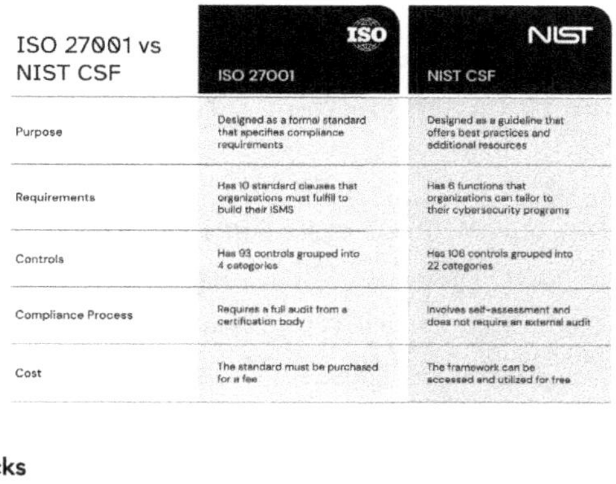

| ISO 27001 vs NIST CSF | ISO 27001 | NIST CSF |
|---|---|---|
| Purpose | Designed as a formal standard that specifies compliance requirements | Designed as a guideline that offers best practices and additional resources |
| Requirements | Has 10 standard clauses that organizations must fulfill to build their ISMS | Has 6 functions that organizations can tailor to their cybersecurity programs |
| Controls | Has 93 controls grouped into 4 categories | Has 106 controls grouped into 22 categories |
| Compliance Process | Requires a full audit from a certification body | Involves self-assessment and does not require an external audit |
| Cost | The standard must be purchased for a fee | The framework can be accessed and utilized for free |

6clicks

Figure 3.2.: Comparison between ISO 27001 and NIST Cybersecurity Framework.

Figure 3.2 compares the International Organization for Standardization 27001 standard and the National Institute of Standards and Technology Cybersecurity Framework. The two security management frameworks demonstrate effective security practices yet have separate objectives, organizational frameworks, and mandatory compliance standards. A third-party audit process requires formal certification per the International Organization for Standardization 27001 standard, which functions as an official compliance framework. Organizations must implement the ten standard clauses while working through ninety-three security controls under four categories. The National Institute of Standards and Technology framework functions primarily as a guide because it lacks the requirements of strict compliance standards. Debugging platforms include six security functions while controlling one hundred and six areas, which are grouped under twenty-two categories. Organizations under the National Institute of Standards and Technology framework perform self-assessments instead of needing external certification that is present in the International Organization for Standardization 27001 standard.

International standards-compliant organizations serving global markets tend to adopt the International Organization for Standardization 27001 due to its official certification process. Various businesses in finance, healthcare, and government entities use this security framework to fulfill their mandatory compliance standards. Organizations that seek adaptable cybersecurity governance tend to select the framework developed by the National Institute of Standards and Technology. Businesses that require organized security frameworks while avoiding external audit responsibilities use this standard in their operations.

The Center for Internet Security Controls is an operational security model accessible for direct implementation. The Center for Internet Security Controls framework stands apart from the International Organization for Standardization 27001 standard and the National Institute of Standards and Technology framework because it provides tools directly for implementing security control. Most organizations select a combination of framework components to build their cybersecurity governance structure as this hybrid model suits regulatory obligations alongside operational demands.

Organizations should choose their cybersecurity framework by considering their security priorities, specific industrial risks, and mandatory compliance requirements. They also need to assess their regulatory exposure before choosing between the International Organization for Standardization 27001 standard and the National Institute of Standards and Technology framework. Businesses handling immediate security needs through easily executable controls will gain the most from the security model provided by the Center for Internet Security Controls.

Security governance effectiveness is determined by continuous assessment, risk-based decision-making, and adherence to business objectives regardless of the chosen framework. The integration of the selected framework needs to continue running through operations alongside periodic evaluation for effectiveness and framework modifications to overcome new security threats. A documented cybersecurity governance framework helps organizations improve security positioning while guarding critical infrastructure and achieving regulatory guidelines.

## 3.2. How to Select the Right Framework for Your Organization

Organizations must select appropriate cybersecurity governance frameworks to achieve security policies that match their business targets while upholding regulatory demands and operational safety needs. They must merge the framework selection process into their current risk management structure and procurement activities. A systematic framework selection system leads organizations to consistently apply security measures to reduce vulnerabilities and integrate governance responsibilities into core business operations.

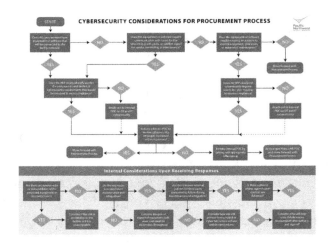

Figure 3.3.: Cybersecurity considerations for the procurement process.

Figure 3.3 illustrates the importance of cybersecurity governance in procurement processes. All organizations must examine security threats from new technological acquisitions, software implementations, and vendor solution setups before using these systems. The procurement evaluation must examine the latest equipment and software for its network integration and data handling abilities and needed security compliance specifications. By conducting this evaluation, organizations can decide what security framework they need to use to control their risks effectively.

Security requirement identification is a fundamental criterion for selecting a framework during procurement operations. Acquiring equipment that links to essential systems and handles confidential data necessitates adopting a compliance-based framework that includes the International Organization for Standardization 27001 standard or the National Institute of Standards and Technology Special Publication 800-171. All these security frameworks enable systematic procedures that check for security threats before system deployment.

A framework must contain essential features that support vendor risk management and continuous monitoring. Organizations must verify that their external service providers fulfill security baseline requirements, including the National Institute of Standards and Technology Special Publication 800-53 and the Secure Controls Framework. When third-party vendors are responsible for critical infrastructure management or maintenance, the selection of a security framework must include continuous vendor monitoring alongside security evaluation criteria.

Internal cybersecurity and procurement teams must

partner when inspecting security procedures linked to new technology acquisitions. Businesses must verify whether security standards appear in procurement documentation, especially proposal requests, and confirm that deployed solution security measures meet their current governance guidelines. This approach integrates security governance into procurement procedures to minimize security risks during new technology deployments.

Companies must approach framework selection as an adaptable operation that depends on ongoing risk evaluations alongside organizational business targets. An organization must regularly evaluate its security governance framework for updates that protect against new threats and technological changes and meet regulatory needs. An adequately organised selection process makes cybersecurity governance strong enough to adapt and maintain resilience while staying aligned with the organization's extended security goals.

## 3.3. Aligning Governance Strategies with Business Objectives

Effectiveness in cybersecurity governance depends on how well its strategies integrate with organizational business targets. Security policies must combine regulatory adherence with substantial contributions toward business strength, process performance, and executive leadership support. An adequately designed governance structure binds cybersecurity into business workflows to meet regulatory requirements and enable growth through innovation by staying compliant.

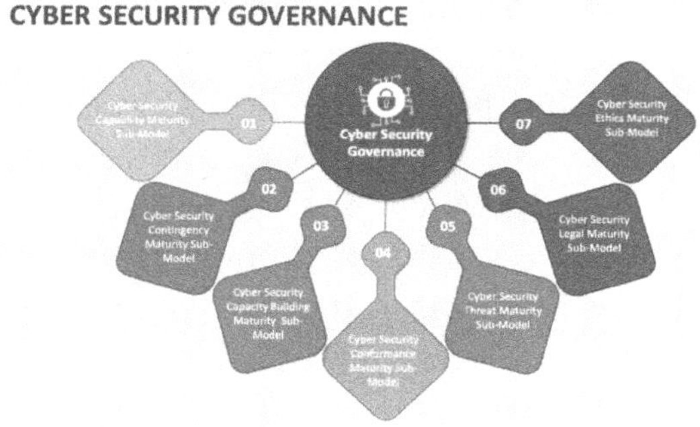

CYBER SECURITY GOVERNANCE

Figure 3.4.: Cybersecurity governance maturity model highlighting key sub-models.

Figure 3.4 presents a structured cybersecurity governance maturity model that outlines essential components organizations must develop to align governance strategies with business goals. A strong security posture emerges from a combination of several governance dimensions that form a cybersecurity system. Security governance develops in response to organizational requirements, regulatory updates, and emerging cyber threats through these fundamental dimensions.

The core element of governance alignment depends on capability maturity since it describes an organization's capacity to evaluate its cybersecurity framework and maintain its continuous development. Organizations that have reached advanced maturity levels combine security governance functions into operational business plans so security initiatives pursue operational targets instead of existing as disconnected compliance activities.

An organization's readiness to handle cyber incidents, business continuity, and disaster recovery plans belongs to the domain of contingency maturity. Every organization needs formal incident response strategies for fast recovery from cyberattacks that reduce operational losses. When business governance systems align with contingency planning, the organization's resilience increases and operational disruptions become shorter during security incidents.

The essential element of capacity-building maturity entails investing in developing cybersecurity abilities, establishing security awareness initiatives, and acquiring technology. Organizations need to train their employees regularly, use better security technologies, and improve employee security understanding to counter escalating cyber threats. They must also establish governance approaches that focus on continuous security instruction, system vulnerability checking, and automation investments to strengthen their defensive capabilities.

Conformance maturity establishes alignment between cybersecurity governance, established standards, organization-specific legal requirements, and contractual obligations. Austere business entities collaborating with highly regulated industries must use their governance systems to fulfill standards, including the International Organization for Standardization 27001 standard, the Health Insurance Portability and Accountability Act, and the General Data Protection Regulation. Organizations achieve full regulatory compliance through complaint maturity, boosting their internal security controls.

Organizations develop threat maturity through their capacity to spot ana, lyze, and actively reduce impending cyber risks. Security frameworks need to combine time-sensitive threat information with persistent monitoring and changeable protective mechanisms, which should act to minimize threats while they remain in an initial stage. Advanced threat maturity organizations utilize artificial intelligence analytics and threat detection automation within their governance approach to speed up responses and enhance defensive capabilities.

Implementing legal maturity makes cybersecurity governance responsible for legal and regulatory compliance requirements. This approach includes properly fulfilling data protection laws, intellectual property security, and contractual obligations regarding cybersecurity risk management. Organizations that focus on legal maturity in their governance structures prevent legal struggles while maintaining security policies that support their corporate legal movements.

Integrating artificial intelligence security tools requires organizations to focus on ethical maturity because these tools enhance cybersecurity governance. Ethical considerations in governance frameworks require security policies and procedures to protect privacy rights and maintain fairness standards, together with accountable data management. The implementation of ethical governance strengthens security decisions through the principles of corporate social responsibility, particularly concerning protecting sensitive customer information.

Comprehensive cybersecurity governance requires executive leadership's direct involvement to align with business core objectives. Chief Information Security Officers maintain vital responsibilities by establishing cybersecurity governance as an essential corporate strategic element while preventing its technical treatment only. Security executives and executive decision-makers form a strategic partnership to guarantee that governance investments keep pace with business expansion requirements along with evolving threats.

The risk-based approach to governance helps organizations make cybersecurity investments through threat-based priority decision-making. Organizations must evaluate risk probabilities and potential damages to properly distribute their security investment funds. Continuous risk assessment integration with adaptive security controls within governance strategies helps organizations stay prepared for evolving security threats and maintain their cybersecurity investments.

A fundamental aspect of governance alignment demands establishing a security-conscious culture across all business units. Development of this culture in organizations requires permanent security awareness programs, detailed incident response plans, and security initiatives that unite different departments. Based on an organizational culture incorporating cybersecurity, the implementation of governance strategies emerges as a proactive operation process that operates systematically within all organizational operations instead of focusing on reactionary compliance methods.

The practice of cybersecurity governance needs to stay flexible to accommodate changes in business operations. Rising security trends from quantum computing, cloud security models, and artificial intelligence-driven threat detection need governance frameworks that support evolving security risks and regulatory adjustments. Organizations keep their cybersecurity governance structure intact through frequent governance reviews, security audits, and compliance assessments.

Organizations must understand cybersecurity governance functions through a dynamic process that advances organizational development. Aligning business objectives with governance strategies enables organizations to develop security postures that promote operational achievement, regulatory compliance, risk mitigation functionality, and trust-based innovation and development.

## 3.4. Q&A Section

Q: What factors matter when choosing a cybersecurity framework?

A: Regulatory needs, risk exposure, operations, and best practices.

Q: How to choose between ISO 27001 and NIST CSF?

A: ISO 27001 suits compliance needs; NIST CSF offers flexibility.

Q: Why align cybersecurity with business goals?

A: It ensures security supports growth, compliance, and risk management.

Q: How can leadership strengthen cybersecurity governance?

A: Prioritize investments, integrate security, and promote awareness.

Q: What are the benefits of a hybrid security framework?

A: It combines compliance (ISO 27001) with flexible risk management (NIST).

Q: How to keep cybersecurity governance effective?

A: Regular audits, risk assessments, and updates to counter new threats.

# 4. Policies, Procedures, and Security Awareness

Cybersecurity policies and procedures are the core elements of organization protection against cyber threats. Well-defined guidelines and operational processes prevent disorganization, exposing systems to intrusions and data breaches while creating non-compliance. Organizations must develop security policies that explain expectations, confidentiality enforcement procedures, and employee training programs for security awareness. The success of cybersecurity governance relies on organized methods of creating policies and implementing procedures and continuous training programs.

The chapter investigates the process of security policy development followed by security procedures deployment across organizational units while analyzing security awareness programs for reducing cyber threats. The research investigates approaches for creating effective governance policies combined with their uniform enforcement and developing a security-focused organizational culture. Security measures and daily operations integration will be emphasized, along with policy implementation hurdles and updated evaluations, to maintain security measures' appropriateness and effectiveness.

## 4.1. Developing Effective Security Policies

A cybersecurity policy is a formal document outlining the organizational strategies to safeguard its assets. The policy creates thorough security objectives, assigns responsibilities, and defines necessary risk reduction procedures. Organizations without effective policy structures enable employees to see security expectations unpredictably, which makes them practice differently and causes more security breaches. When organizations neglect to build proper security policies, they face multiple challenges, including non-compliance with regulations, operational weaknesses, and a lack of accountability.

Business goal alignment requires security policies that deliver precise instructions and ensure compliance. Such policies present implementation challenges because they need interpretation, while too strict policies create productivity obstacles. Security policy documentation must clearly outline what daily operations can and cannot do regarding acceptable usage guidelines, data protection policies, and response protocols. Security policies must adjust to new threats by undergoing regular reviews, which lead to necessary policy updates. Old policies both increase compliance challenges and create opportunities for attackers to develop fresh methods of assault. Security policies must follow regulatory requirements for organizations to maintain full regulatory compliance while protecting themselves from legal consequences. The industry best practices described in ISO 27001, NIST 800-53, and GDPR are guidelines that direct policy development processes. Organizations operating in heavily regulated sectors need their security policies to include risk assessments, data encryption requirements, and required security monitoring methods that fulfill industry exceptional standards. The absence of regulatory alignment would result in security policies being unable to deliver the necessary protection against legal liabilities and operational risks.

Multiple core elements form security policies to handle different aspects of cybersecurity management. Business organizations must establish the security policies illustrated in the image to safeguard their digital resources. These policies comprise the rules that secure data, manage access control, and establish threat response standards.

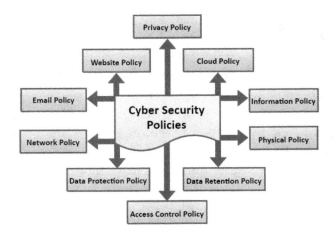

Figure 4.1.: Key types of cybersecurity policies in an organization.

The strategic importance of these policies creates a foundation for complete organizational security protection. Implementing an access control policy allows specific users who meet authorization standards to access sensitive data and systems, thus blocking unauthorized people from causing damaging data breaches. The data protection policy applies security measures for encryption and data classification requirements while specifying information retention rules to defend sensitive data from unauthorized access. Implementing network security policies relies on deploying firewalls alongside intrusion detection systems to maintain secure network configurations that fight external security threats. Workers must follow established email security policies about communication handling to prevent phishing and social engineering attacks. Implementing cloud security policies safeguards cloud computing remote environments by defending them from unauthorized access and protecting data from leaks. Strict policy enforcement remains essential for achieving an organization's goal of maintaining a solid cybersecurity position.

Well-designed security policies must integrate existing structured cybersecurity frameworks as these systems allow organizations to manage their cybersecurity risks systematically. Security authorities consider the National Institute of Standards and Technology (NIST) Cybersecurity Framework one of the most popular standardized approaches to security governance management. A framework defines five critical functions: Identify, Protect, Detect, Respond, and Recover. The defined categories serve organizations as operational guidelines for risk reduction through security policy implementation, which builds more substantial cyber defense capabilities.

| Identify | Protect | Detect | Respond | Recover |
|---|---|---|---|---|
| Asset Management | Access Control | Anomalies and Events | Response Planning | Recovery Planning |
| Business Environment | Awareness and Training | | Communications | |
| Governance | Data Security | Security Continuous Monitoring | Analysis | Improvements |
| Risk Assessment | Info Protection Processes and Procedures | | Mitigation | |
| | Maintenance | Detection Processes | | Communications |
| Risk Management Strategy | Protective Technology | | Improvements | |

Figure 4.2.: The NIST Cybersecurity Framework and its core security functions.

All functions within the framework contribute to the policy development process. Organizations use the Identify function to identify their assets, business environment requirements, governance needs, and risk management strategy. A cybersecurity policy must outline the assets for protection before establishing any protective measures. Security controls ranging from access control to data protection and employee awareness constitute the core elements of the Protect function. A comprehensive cybersecurity policy's essential components serve to train employees, protect sensitive information, and control system access.

Security analytics, continuous monitoring, and anomaly detection run as the core of the Detect function. A security policy must establish immediate threat surveillance systems that detect impending cyber threats before transitioning to critical security failures. Organizational awareness about security breaches occurs after significant damage happens when monitoring strategies are not effectively established. The Respond function specifies incident response planning together with communications and mitigation strategies. Organizations must establish a comprehensive policy framework outlining their incident response plan, containment measures, forensic examination, and regulatory compliance requirements. Organizations that implement the Recover function establish plans for recovering operations after incidents and develop continuous improvement processes for ongoing security enhancement.

Security policies that use the NIST Cybersecurity Framework produce a step-by-step process for governing security through standardized procedures. Each framework function should include corresponding policies to aid comprehensive risk management initiatives. Access control policies must link to the Protect and Identify functions to establish authorized system access restrictions for personnel. Incident response procedures require alignment with the Respond and Recover functions to deliver instructions that help contain, analyze, and recover from cyber-attacks.

Security policies become effective when proper enforcement procedures exist. Enforcement systems must be present in security approaches because theoretical guidelines alone cannot function as a security measure. Security policies must become integral to regular organizational work so employees fully understand all security requirements. The combination of identifying and granting access through (IAM) systems, endpoint security methods, and SIEM platforms enables organizations to monitor policy adherence actively and instantly recognize violations. Security audits must run regularly to measure compliance standards and locate weak spots, making policy procedures more effective.

Organizations must maintain employee training and awareness programs because they appropriately support policy compliance efforts. Well-defined security policies become useless when employees disregard them. Every organization needs to perform standard cybersecurity training because it teaches team members about best security practices, new threats, and official policy changes. Security policies become more effective through simulated phishing tests, security drills, and hands-on workshops, which help employees reduce security breaches that arise from human mistakes.

Security policies require periodic revisions to match progressed threats, regulatory alterations, and technological evolution. When policy frameworks remain static, organizations are exposed to new attack methods that emerge in the market. Companies need to develop a policy review method that includes security teams, compliance officers, and business representatives. The policy must be edited whenever security regulations, performance guidelines, or business operations are modified to preserve its operational worth.

Pursuing security policies requires organizations to find an equilibrium between ensuring business operations do not suffer from security measures. Security teams must confirm that their established policies avoid creating obstacles that limit operational productivity. Security policies must utilize a risk-based method so organizations can prioritize critical security controls without causing interruptions to everyday operational activities. Organizations achieve effective practical security policies when department heads join forces with IT teams and compliance officers during policy creation. Security policies protect an organization's cybersecurity strategy through their defined risk management protocols, incident response procedures, and compliance requirements. Organizations can implement strong cybersecurity measures by integrating security framework alignment to policies and automated enforcement along with policy review procedures. An organization must implement both detailed security policies and organized frameworks, in addition to ongoing monitoring, to properly safeguard sensitive assets while meeting regulatory standards in modern, complex cyber threat conditions.

# 4.2. Implementing Security Procedures Across Business Units

The foundation of security objectives depends on policies, yet the achievement of those objectives follows established procedures. Implementing security procedures interprets policy requirements into operational steps that direct employees, IT personnel, and management in security implementation. Security documentation deficiencies produce inconsistent security enforcement, raising the chance of security misconfiguration, unauthorized access, and regulatory non-compliance.

Each business unit needs its security procedures to match its operational requirements. Different departments inside organizations have distinct security requirements since IT requirements vary from those of human resources and finance branches. IT departments concentrate on network security, vulnerability management, and access control, while other business units need to follow procedures for secure data handling, compliance reporting, and risk protection. Every organization needs role-based security procedures to teach staff members their duties regarding protecting corporate assets.

Developing a comprehensive security procedure requires covering four essential areas: risk assessment, access control enforcement, monitoring and auditing, and employee training. An organization's security stance depends on completing all procedure steps. When business units lack standardized security procedures, they develop irregular security methods that result in entry points for attackers.

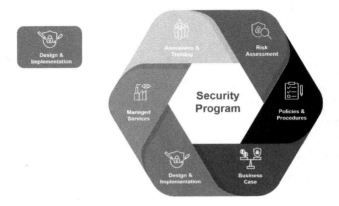

Figure 4.3.: Security program components for implementing security procedures.

The security program shows the fundamental elements that produce successful security procedure executions. To implement security procedures successfully, the framework must integrate policies and procedures with awareness and training, risk assessment, business case analysis, managed services, design, and implementation. All components work together to develop security procedures that are structured effectively for proper communication and enforcement purposes.

Initial security procedures require performing a complete risk assessment. The primary function of risk assessment involves detecting security dangers while measuring vulnerability effects for different business areas. Security controls derive from the results established through risk assessment processes. Organizations' absence of regular risk assessments leads them to deploy ineffective security measures against current security threats. Security teams who regularly perform risk analysis maintain the ability to stop new threats as they develop so incidents stay under control.

The next step is to create policies and procedures explaining the implementation approach for security controls. All security procedures require detailed instructions for handling sensitive data, user access control and encryption protocols, and strategies for handling security incidents. Every business unit must grasp its applicable security procedures to demonstrate conformity with the enterprise security guidelines.

Organizations need security training for employees because it helps maintain security procedures effectively. Security procedures remain ineffective when employees lack sufficient training because they represent the main vulnerability for organizations in cybersecurity systems. Organizations must supply security awareness instruction, phishing simulation activities, and hands-on training sessions for worker education regarding security procedure compliance. The security teams need to establish simple guidance documents that explain how staff members can perform security tasks effectively.

Most organizations face significant difficulties when their employees resist implementing security procedures. Security controls that discomfort staff members during implementation may become disregarded by users who choose to work around these measures. Workers' implementation of non-standard work methods creates new security risks for the organization.

To overcome this problem, security teams must make security procedures work perfectly with business procedures. Security systems based on automated solutions like identity and access management (IAM), together with single sign-on (SSO) and endpoint detection and response (EDR), simplify security enforcement without interrupting operational workflow structures.

Security procedures need the deployment of managed services to function effectively. MSSPs offer their clients continuous monitoring, threat intelligence services, and incident response capabilities. Organizations that do not maintain their own cybersecurity talents can use managed services to successfully implement their security protocols. Security services provide immediate visibility into security events alongside prompt incident detection and reduction capabilities.

Security procedures need to remain active documents instead of static ones. They need ongoing evaluation to ensure their effectiveness before organizations modify them to confront new security threats. Organizations need to conduct regular security audits and incident review procedures to check if their current security procedures deliver proper defense. Security procedures require assessment for their effectiveness to determine security control enhancements that will boost protection standards. Security professionals conduct routine assessments like penetration tests and vulnerability check-ups, which deliver critical information about security procedure performance.

All security procedures need to become automatic whenever automation technologies are available. Manual procedures show frequent inconsistencies because they are vulnerable to errors from human handlers. Security automation tools enable organizations to identify policy breaches while making automatic corrections. Organization-wide consistent security enforcement depends on Security information and event management (SIEM) systems, automated compliance scanners, and behavioral analytics tools working together.

A security documentation system that allows simple employee access should exist for all security procedures. A central knowledge platform and internal security website grant employees access to the latest security protocols, standard operating procedures (SOPs), and incident response protocols. Security documentation must undergo periodic evaluation to display modified security directions, new threat options, and new regulatory limits.

Executive backing is the fundamental requirement for implementing security procedures since it secures essential funding and provides resources. Business units do not enforce security requirements when executives fail to prioritize security. Security teams must collaborate with senior management to effectively implement security procedures as a part of the organization's business strategies and risk management approaches.

Security procedure frameworks must contain key performance indicators that help organizations track their security compliance and effectiveness levels. Security performance tracking depends on measurements consisting of security incident counts, policy violation detection, and employee training involvement. Real-time monitoring enabled by security dashboards and reporting tools informs users about current compliance metrics while indicating locations that need enhanced security measures.

Security procedure deployment in business units demands a methodical process that handles risk assessment, policy enforcement education, learning, automatic system enhancements, and nonstop monitoring. Without proper implementation of these essential components, security procedures become either nonfunctional or inconsistent. Organizations can boost their security by integrating security procedures into daily business operations, managed security services, and automated enforcement systems.

# 4.3. Building a Security-First Culture Through Awareness Programs

Cyber security exists beyond technological aspects since human beings are its vital components. A security culture establishes active protection efforts from employees at all levels, including management teams. Establishing such a culture needs ongoing effort rather than a single isolated attempt. Security development depends on assessing your security's current state and requires organizational goal-setting accompanied by ongoing progress assessment and continuous improvement initiatives. The security culture design follows the pattern presented in the attached figure.

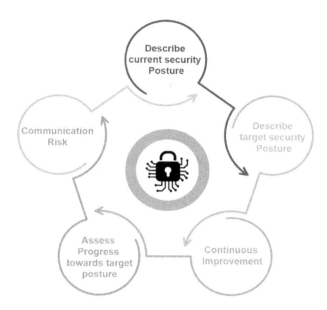

Figure 4.4.: The continuous process of improving security culture.

To begin the process, organizations must describe their existing security situation. Organizations must analyze employee security methods and determine weak areas and past failures. The assessment of employee performance regarding security policy implementation, along with the use of robust passwords and their ability to spot phishing threats, must be established. Organizations cannot enhance performance when they remain unaware of their present conditions.

Organizations need to establish specific security parameters that will serve as their targets. They must also create specific expectations and stipulate compliance objectives and security protocols. Leadership needs to establish organizational security requirements before sharing them with workforce members. Organizations should create performance-based security goals, including decreased phishing success rates and better adoption of multi-factor authentication systems.

The achievement of a target security posture depends heavily on the effectiveness of security awareness programs. Workers require training materials that catch their interest and directly correspond to their job responsibilities. Long generic courses about security prove ineffective for securing proper results. Security best practices gain deeper retention through interactive training combining real-world simulation practices and phishing tests. Posture improvement requires straightforward security policies that users can easily follow.

Measuring progress is critical. An organization needs to monitor employee compliance with security protocols and analyze the effectiveness of implemented training programs. Security teams use phishing simulations, compliance audits, and behavior analytics to monitor progress. Employee failure to avoid phishing attempts and security alert neglect requires training protocol revision.

Continuous improvement is essential. Organizations need their security culture to adapt to each developing cyber threat. Companies must conduct regular policy updates, followed by fresh training content and implementation of employee feedback. Security teams need to always keep up with emerging threats since they must develop new protective measures against upcoming risks.

Furthermore, organizations must address all communication-related security problems. Employee security concerns will stay hidden when they feel reluctant to report such matters. An organization with a security-first mindset enables staff to freely discuss cybersecurity-related topics. Staff members should possess clear reporting protocols for detecting unusual activities yet face no reprimands.

Developing a security culture requires organizations to dedicate prolonged efforts. The process begins with evaluating the present situation, followed by goal definition, employee education, and measurement of advancement and continuous improvement. Properly implementing security understanding methods enables organizations to create daily security practices that lower potential risks while fortifying their protection systems.

## 4.4. Q&A Section

Q: What is the purpose of security policies?

A: They define objectives, responsibilities, and enforcement for managing risks.

Q: Why align security policies with regulations?

A: Compliance prevents legal issues and meets industry standards.

Q: How to enforce security procedures?

A: Use automation, monitoring, and regular audits.

Q: Why do awareness programs fail?

A: They lack engagement, frequency, and interactive learning.

Q: How does leadership impact security?

A: Strong leadership drives compliance and security culture.

# Part II.

# Risk Management – Identifying and Mitigating Threats

# 5. The Cyber Risk Landscape

Modern cyber risks continue to transform quickly because organizations must now deal with advanced threats that compromise operations, release private information, and lead to monetary loss. Organizations face different levels of cyber threats, which include ransomware, advanced persistent threats, and complex supply chain attacks. Organizations need complete knowledge of these threats to create efficient security measures. A comprehensive analysis of major cyber threats occurs while explaining the significance of conducting business impact analysis and reviewing essential insights gained from notable cyber incidents.

## 5.1. Understanding Cyber Threats: Ransomware, APTs, Supply Chain Attacks

Modern cyber threats continue to develop techniques that seek out organizations regardless of size or industry. Terrorists employ advanced yet complex methods to breach computer systems before they steal crucial information and cause operational breakdowns. The present cyber environment features three main malicious attacks: ransomware, advanced persistent threats (APTs), and supply chain attacks. Organizations require an understanding of destructive cyber threats to build effective cybersecurity measures.

Ransomware exists as one of the worst threats in terms of its financial impact on cyberattacks. This malicious software locks user files before they require payment, leading to operational interruptions and extensive financial consequences. Cybercriminals distribute ransomware through deceptive email messages, dangerous file attachments, and unsecured exploit tools that exploit security gaps on unpatched systems. After its activation, ransomware causes a fast spread that encrypts essential systems before requesting cryptocurrency payments to gain access again. Most vital infrastructure organizations, healthcare entities, and financial institutions surrender ransom payments to regain system access but experience no assurance of data recovery and create opportunities for additional cyber-attacks.

Organizations should protect themselves from ransomware through the use and combination of multiple security protection systems. Endpoint detection and response (EDR), secure backup methods, continuous security update installation, and complete personnel training sessions make up essential defensive measures. The principle of least privilege (PoLP) should be applied by organizations to control user access to sensitive systems because it minimizes environmental damage when attackers infiltrate their networks.

Well-funded groups of nation-state actors and organized cybercriminal entities perform long-term stealthy cyber attacks known as Advanced persistent threats (APTs). Traditional malware's detection ability falls short compared to APT techniques because it employs complex methods to remain undetected while sustaining lengthy unauthorized network access. Zero-day vulnerabilities, social engineering, and credential theft methods allow attackers to stealthily penetrate their targets, who stay undetected for months or even years.

APT operations focus on three key goals: cyber espionage, intellectual property theft, and destructive attacks on essential infrastructure. Threat actors use specific malware, custom backdoors, and encrypted command-and-control channels for their attacks because standard security technologies cannot identify these methods. Organizations must assume a preventative stance against APTs by dividing their networks while keeping advanced detection systems active through ongoing monitoring, implementing tight identity control protocols, and sharing threat intelligence data.

Supply chain attacks have evolved into a significant cybersecurity vulnerability that allows attackers to infiltrate organizations by attacking their third-party vendors, service providers, and software suppliers. The interconnected business ecosystems provide attackers with an advantage due to which organizations struggle to recognize threats until they reach multiple points in their network. Supply chain attacks differ from standard cyberattacks because they invade approved vendors to integrate malicious content into legitimate software updates, cloud offerings, or product parts.

The SolarWinds breach became a primary example of a supply chain attack when criminals compromised regularly used software updates from the IT management platform. Through this attack method, hackers obtained entry for thousands of organizations, including government departments and Fortune 500 companies. In 2021, ransomware was delivered to numerous businesses through Kaseya's trusted IT management software because cybercriminals took advantage of its security gaps.

Figure 5.1.: ENISA report on the growing impact of supply chain attacks.

Gateway attacks have become more prevalent recently, as revealed by the European Union Agency for Cybersecurity (ENISA), which shows attackers exploit weaknesses in program code, take advantage of supplier-trusting customers, and perform malicious software injections. As shown in Figure 5.1, 66 percent of supply chain attacks focus on vulnerabilities within the supplier's code, while 62 percent rely on malware to infect systems. Attackers use trust in suppliers through their tactics and techniques in 62 percent of cases, while data exfiltration stands as the primary objective in 58 percent of attacks.

A successful security approach for supply chain risk reduction must employ thorough vendor risk control, software integrity confirmation, and persistent monitoring of dependent third-party systems. Organizations must perform security evaluations on vendors, followed by mandatory access control implementation and installation of zero-trust security systems. Organizations must deploy cryptographic signatures to check software update authenticity before releasing them for deployment.

Since cyber threats constantly develop new methods, security remains an ongoing battle which organizations must address. Organizations must proactively improve their security approaches to deal with new threats. An organization must combine regular security evaluations with rigorous update management and employee security understanding programs alongside real-time security analysis to defend against cyber threats. Organizations can develop better resilience to handle escalating cyber threats through proper threat management of ransomware along with APTs and supply chain attacks.

## 5.2. Business Impact Analysis for Cyber Risks

Every organization needs business impact analysis to determine the effects of cyber risks on their operations. Next-generation security threats expand daily, so businesses must evaluate their exposed areas and measure their financial and operational risks before creating plans to handle potential harm. Organizations experience significant operational disturbances in addition to regulatory sanctions rep, reputation damage, and financial loss following cyber incidents. Evaluating how different online threats interrupt essential corporate processes allows organizations to develop an intellectual framework for continuous operations and operational stability.

The first step of a business impact analysis requires organizations to determine which business operations are most vital and identify how cyber threats can affect them. Critical systems, vital applications, and stored data need protection for operational continuity. Ransoming vital business files through an attack would trigger the encryption of sensitive files, which in turn causes critical business interruptions. Disclosure of confidential customer data through data breaches triggers regulatory sanctions and trust-related business losses. Supply chain attacks spread past the borders of individual organizations to disrupt numerous industries throughout their networks. A comprehensive cybersecurity plan requires understanding serious risks and attack scenario probabilities.

A financial disaster results from all cyber threats. Organizations must pay ransoms and fees from regulators and lawyers and spend money to restore their systems. Corporate reputational harm and customer defection combined with business prospects disappear, resulting in indirect costs that commonly surpass direct financial losses. Large-scale cyber attacks will scare organizations into financial harm that could persist for years. To offset financial damages from cyber attacks, businesses must determine their resilience to cyber losses through risk mitigation approaches, including cyber insurance with advanced defense systems and secure backup systems.

Incident response planning is a fundamental part of business impact analysis. A well-structured response plan includes clear containment measures, communication protocols, and recovery strategies. Organizations must ensure that security teams and executives understand their roles during a cyber attack. Recovery efforts should focus on restoring systems quickly, minimizing downtime, and protecting data integrity. Without a structured incident response plan, businesses risk prolonged disruptions and increased financial and reputational losses.

Cyber threats have significantly impacted businesses in recent years. The following table summarizes major cyber attacks in the United States in 2023 and 2024, including their impact and key lessons learned.

## Table 5.1.: Major Cyber Attacks and Their Impact in the USA (2023-2024)

| Date | Victim | Attack Type | Impact (Loss in $) | Lessons Learned |
|---|---|---|---|---|
| Nov 21, 2024 | Blue Yonder | Ransomware (Termite) | 2.5M | Strengthen backups, improve ransomware defenses |
| Dec 3, 2024 | BT | Ransomware (Black Basta) | 3.1M | Enhance endpoint security, improve phishing training |
| Dec 16, 2024 | Texas Tech Univ. | Ransomware (Interlock) | 1.2M | Increase MFA usage, strengthen network segmentation |
| Dec 30, 2024 | Cisco | Data Breach (IntelBroker) | 5.8M | Strengthen network segmentation, improve encryption |
| Feb 12, 2024 | Change Healthcare | Ransomware Attack | 4.0M | Regular patching, stronger access controls |
| 2024 | Evolve Bank | Data Breach | 6.5M | Improve encryption, adopt zero-trust models |

The examples represent the danger level of cyber security threats. Ransomware is an especially destructive cyber attack type that leads organizations to suffer monetary damages and service interruptions, except for customer information breaches, which trigger legal penalties alongside severe damage to the company's reputation. Supply chain attacks penetrate multiple organizations through third-party vendor networks, becoming a rising threat to organizations. Organizations without proactive cybersecurity measures usually face significant challenges when attempting to rebound after encountering these risks.

Business impact analysis requires a complete comprehension of cyber attacks' severity because it helps organizations identify their potential impacts. Recent cyber attacks in the United States resulted in diverse operational disruption and financial impact, as shown in this visual presentation.

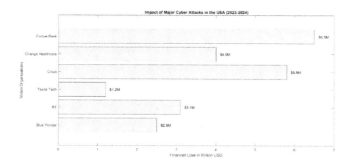

Figure 5.2.: Impact of Major Cyber Attacks in the USA (2023-2024)

Risk assessment of exposure must remain continuous as a fundamental requirement for organizations looking to develop a more assertive cybersecurity posture. The ransomware incident at Change Healthcare resulted in a 4.0 million dollar financial loss and severe healthcare services disruptions, demonstrating the absolute requirement for systems that maintain business operations throughout cyber emergencies. Because of these substantial financial losses, organizations must assess their cybersecurity strategies through ongoing reviews to prevent future threats.

Organizations need to deploy security measures ahead of time to reduce risks and decrease business damage. The decision-making process relies on business impact analysis to make sure security spending matches the main dangers organizations face. Organizations need to prioritize cyber resilience, which requires constant surveillance, real-time threat recognition, and quick action capabilities to meet the elevated financial risks. A single attack with Black Basta ransomware harmed BT's operations by causing 72 hours of service outages, which stood as evidence of ransomware incidents' extensive impacts on operational efficiency and customer trust.

Reducing business impact requires employee training regarding cybersecurity best practices as a main priority. Security breaches originate from human errors; phishing attacks cause more than ninety percent of all data breaches yearly. Employees without proper training risk encountering phishing attacks, credential theft, and malware infections. Information-driven employees act as the primary protective barrier against cyber attacks. Organizations must conduct simulated attacks and hands-on training and distribute regular security updates through awareness programs because this approach helps employees understand their essential role in preventing attacks.

Businesses must conduct impact analysis because regulations are essential in determining their decision-making process. Organizations which do not conform to security regulations will endure severe financial consequences. The General Data Protection Regulation (GDPR) includes two potential penalties for companies in violation. Hence, they face maximum fines either at 4% of their global annual turnover or €20 million, whichever value exceeds the other. Similarly, the California Consumer Privacy Act (CCPA) mandates fines of up to 2,500 per unintentional violation and 7,500 for intentional violations. Only achieving compliance enables organizations to defend their reputation while ensuring financial stability and meeting legal requirements. Inadequate regulatory compliance makes businesses vulnerable to legal actions, customers lose trust, and operating rules may forbid them from conducting business in specific regions.

Continuous effort goes into updating and improving the effectiveness of a business impact analysis to achieve success. Organizations face continuous development in cyber threats while new system security weaknesses appear daily. Organizations must maintain a constant readiness to check their security position while changing their response plans to threats. Security leaders need to perform constant risk assessments, penetration testing, and security audits to confirm their cybersecurity methods' effectiveness. Protecting sensitive data becomes more effective through zero-trust security concepts, which enforce recurring checks on users and devices trying to access this information.

The damaging effects of cyber threats on organizations surpass any possibility of dismissal. Organizations need to actively identify their security risks, followed by strong security implementation practices and comprehensive response planning. When organizations disregard their cyber threats as purely IT problems, all components of an organization face business risks. Organizations can respond effectively to cyber threats in a hostile environment through complete business impact analyses, simultaneously allowing them to plan for worst-case scenarios.

# 5.3. Case Study: High-Profile Cyber Attacks and Lessons Learned

Understanding actual cyber attacks enables organizations to gain essential knowledge about system weaknesses, attacker approaches, and security defense capabilities. The following section examines three significant cyber incidents that deliver key organizational learning points.

Over 200,000 systems in 150 nations fell victim to the 2017 WannaCry ransomware cyber assault, which encrypted their data. An un-updated Microsoft Windows security flaw enabled the cyber attack to target multiple institutions within businesses, hospitals, and governmental departments. The key takeaway from this lesson was that patching processes should happen immediately. Organizations need to deploy security updates immediately since doing so blocks potential attacks on discovered vulnerabilities. The economic impact from this incident reached between 2 and 4 billion dollars across the businesses affected.

The SolarWinds supply chain attack from 2020 enabled hackers to corrupt SolarWinds software updates with malware, which infected thousands of organizations spanning Fortune 500 firms and government agencies. The cybersecurity breach revealed organizations' security dangers in their software supply networks. Organizations must conduct security evaluations of their vendors to protect their systems and track software reliability while applying zero-trust protection models. The monetary damage from this cyber assault reached between 100 million and 200 million dollars because organizations needed to recover lost data along with downed systems and data compromise costs.

The Colonial Pipeline ransomware attack in 2021 resulted in fuel shortages across the United States after cybercriminals used compromised credentials to infiltrate the system. The incident emphasized the need for robust access controls, multi-factor authentication, and network segmentation to limit ransomware spread. The Colonial Pipeline attack disrupted fuel supplies for several days, leading to an estimated 5 million dollars in ransom payments and significant financial losses in operational downtime and lost revenue.

The following table summarizes the financial impact of these high-profile cyber attacks, showing the monetary loss and the affected sectors.

Table 5.2.: Financial Impact of High-Profile Cyber Attacks

| Date | Cyber Attack | Impact (Loss in $) | Downtime (Days) | Affected Sectors |
|---|---|---|---|---|
| May 2017 | WannaCry Ransomware | 4B | 1-2 | Healthcare, Finance, Govt |
| Dec 2020 | SolarWinds Attack | 100-200M | 7-10 | Govt, IT, Telecom |
| May 2021 | Colonial Pipeline | 5M | 5-7 | Energy, Transport |

This type of cyber threat incident represents its serious nature. Cyber attacks through ransomware consistently rank among the most destructive threats since they result in financial loss and operational disruptions. Data breaches sacrifice sensitive customer information, leading to legal penalties and damaging corporate reputations. Multiple organizations risk attacks through supply chain attacks because hackers target third-party vendors in these assaults, which makes these threats increasingly significant. A proactive cybersecurity strategy becomes essential because organizations that do not predict security risks experience difficulties in their recovery process.

Businesses must fully grasp the seriousness of cyber assaults to perform accurate business impact analysis. Recent cyber attacks throughout the United States have led to different levels of financial loss and operational disturbances, as illustrated in the following figure.

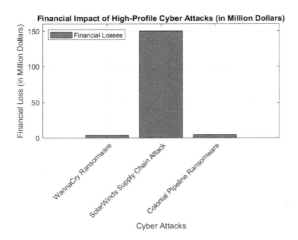

Figure 5.3.: Notable cyber attacks and their impact on industries.

As seen from this visual evidence, organizations must

perform ongoing risk assessments to protect themselves against cyber attacks. The ransomware attack against Change Healthcare demonstrated how it caused four million dollars in financial damages and extensive breakdown of healthcare operations, thus underscoring the imperative to establish systems that continue functioning through cyber emergencies. Organizations must periodically assess their cybersecurity strategies and study emerging threats to prevent future security risks.

Business protection requires organizations to deploy strategic security methods that reduce potential risks and operational impacts. The process of business impact analysis directs decision-making by matching security funding to the most important security threats. High financial risks force organizations to maintain cyber resilience while monitoring threats continuously in real-time and developing prompt response actions. The Black Basta ransomware attack caused BT to suffer 72 hours of disrupted service, negatively impacting operational effectiveness and customer trust.

Employees need to undergo essential cybersecurity training to help decrease business-related disturbances. People continue to commit errors at work that cause security breaches, and phishing attacks lead to more than 90% of data leaks. Unprepared staff members are likelier to fall for phishing schemes and encounter credential theft and malware contamination incidents. Organizations with knowledgeable staff members function as their frontline protection against cyber attacks. Security awareness programs must contain simulated attacks, hands-on training, and regular security update sessions to strengthen best practices. Hence, employees properly recognize their protective roles against these attacks.

Business impact analysis depends extensively on regulatory compliance regulations. Organizations which violate security regulations will encounter significant penalties from authorities. Companies that break GDPR must pay fines amounting to the higher value between 4% of their global annual revenue and €20 million. Similarly, the California Consumer Privacy Act (CCPA) mandates fines of up to 2,500 per unintentional violation and 7,500 for intentional violations. Organizations must comply with regulations because this requirement protects their financial operations and reputation while providing necessary safety measures. Companies that fail to satisfy regulatory standards face higher possibilities of legal action while customers lose trust, and operating bans apply to selected markets.

A successful business impact analysis depends on continuously revising its components and features; daily, the digital landscape experiences permanent evolution through newly developed vulnerabilities. Businesses have to stay alert while conducting constant security posture evaluations that lead them to implement suitable incident response adjustments. Security leaders should regularly assess network risk pen, penetration testing, and security audits to verify ongoing cybersecurity effectiveness. The zero-trust security model provides additional protection benefits because it demands continuous user and device authentication for accessing critical data records.

Business operations face excessive damage from cyber threats that organizations cannot dismiss. Organizations need to conduct active risk assessments, followed by robust implementation of security measures and creation of powerful response protocols. Cyber threats need to be regarded as business risks rather than solely as IT problems since they impact all organizational functions. Business organizations that perform adequate impact analysis preparation become more resistant to cyber threats across their operations in this vulnerable digital environment.

## 5.4. Q&A Section

Q: What are the biggest cyber threats?

A: Ransomware, APTs, and supply chain attacks.

Q: How to prevent ransomware?

A: Use security tools, backups, and employee training.

Q: Why is business impact analysis important?

A: It protects assets and ensures quick recovery.

Q: What do major cyber attacks teach?

A: Patch systems, secure vendors, and improve response.

Q: How to secure the supply chain?

A: Vet vendors, limit access, and use zero-trust.

# 6. Risk Assessment and Mitigation Strategies

Risk assessment establishes itself as an essential operational procedure to find and study threats that endanger business assets, operational processes, and strategic business goals. Through this method, organizations better understand their weak points while lowering their susceptibility to threats. Business continuance depends on effective risk management because it can secure assets and meet regulatory requirements. The chapter uses risk assessment methodologies by detailing the qualitative and quantitative methods before presenting the ISO 27005 framework and FAIR model framework in risk management practice. This subsection will cover the development process to produce an effective risk treatment plan for reducing identified risks.

# 6.1. Risk Assessment Methodologies: Qualitative vs. Quantitative

A cybersecurity strategy needs risk assessment to function properly. By performing risk assessment, organizations can detect security threats, evaluate their nature, and find options to reduce their impact on system confidentiality, integrity, and operation availability. Preventing and reducing cyber threat impacts serves as the primary goal to avoid financial loss, legal penalties, and damage to reputation. Cyber threat risk assessment includes identifying the chances of attacks and determining their possible consequences. Qualitative and quantitative analysis are the two main approaches organizations use for risk assessment. Risk assessment methods have essential parts in identification processes, although their assessment approaches and required information differ, as well as their generated results.

## 6.1.1. Qualitative Risk Analysis in Cybersecurity

Security risks are evaluated during qualitative risk analysis by applying subjective assessment methods to discover their character and possible effects. The risk assessment method establishes order by identifying risks for initial treatment decisions. Risk evaluation during qualitative analysis requires assigning ratings based on probability and consequences through standard categories like high, medium, and low. The main advantage of qualitative analysis lies in its fast and low data requirements, rendering it useful, particularly for organizations with limited resources or those just starting their risk management development.

The cyber security team establishes a high likelihood of phishing attack occurrence because attackers commonly employ social engineering tactics. An organization implementing thorough email protection and staff education about security will experience a medium risk level during such incidents. A ransomware attack presents a high risk because both the potential to occur and the potential damage it causes are significant, especially when organizations maintain insufficient backup measures and outdated security infrastructure.

Equality-based risk analysis standards, including risk matrices or heat maps, assist cybersecurity teams to group risks and identify vital ones that need immediate resolution. Organizations typically use risk matrices for visual evaluation to examine potential organizational effects versus the estimated risk frequency. A distributed denial-of-service (DDoS) attack qualifies as medium likelihood and medium impact according to risk assessment schemes, which indicates that standard security measures can effectively counter such attacks.

Qualitative analysis provides a general overview of the cybersecurity risk landscape, allowing teams to focus on high-priority risks before they move to more detailed analysis.

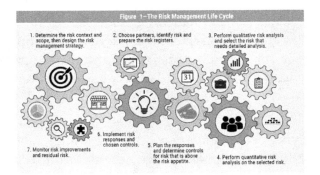

Figure 6.1.: Risk Management Life Cycle in Cybersecurity

Figure 6.1 illustrates the risk management life cycle, highlighting the early stages where qualitative risk analysis helps identify and categorize potential risks. The cycle proceeds with further detailed analysis using other tools like quantitative assessments, as shown in the life cycle process.

## 6.1.2. Quantitative Risk Analysis in Cybersecurity

Risk analysis at its quantitative level requires assigning numerical measures to risks along with their likelihood and impact factors for exact measurement. The method bases its predictions on statistical data by studying historical information through simulations or calculations to determine potential monetary and operational impacts due to risks. Organizations use this approach to request cybersecurity budget support and review potential payment losses from security risks.

Quantitative risk analysis performs financial loss projections in cases of data breaches by assembling data regarding regulatory fines and legal fees, recovery expenses, and customer attrition resulting from reputation damage. Through this data, the organization gains accurate insight into its risk cost to make resource allocation decisions for risk reduction purposes.

One core quantitative risk analysis method relies on Monte Carlo simulation to develop numerous simulated results from multiple risk variables through statistical modeling. Organizations use this approach to calculate the financial effects of cyber dangers through simulations that run multiple different risk scenarios. The total cost of a ransomware attack can be estimated with Monte Carlo simulations through analysis of ransom expenses, restoration expenditures, and business revenue losses sustained during systems being offline.

Calculating data breach expenses related to customer records functions as an additional quantitative analytical approach. The assessment evaluates elements, including damaged customer numbers and expenses, to notify subscribers of legal expenses and GDPR-related monetary penalties. The exact measurement of security-related expenses through quantitative analysis enables organizations to make informed investment choices regarding their cybersecurity programs.

Quantitative analysis provides a detailed understanding of the objective nature of identifying risks. However, it requires extensive data access and additional time to process. Quantitative analysis becomes essential for organizations that require data-based decision-making and ROI assessments for cybersecurity expenditures.

Figure 6.2.: Comparison of Quantitative and Qualitative Risk Analysis in Cybersecurity

Figure 6.2 shows the comparison between qualitative and quantitative approaches in cybersecurity. As seen in the figure, qualitative analysis is typically subjective and used to identify risks early on. In contrast, quantitative analysis offers detailed, data-driven insights into the potential financial consequences of specific risks.

## 6.1.3. Integrating Both Methods in Cybersecurity Risk Management

Organizations gain complete cybersecurity risk management by effectively integrating qualitative risk assessment with quantitative risk analysis techniques. Organizations that utilize qualitative analysis to group and rank risks create better risk prioritization according to impact severity and probability rates. After risk identification occurs, organizations can strengthen their quantitative assessments to reveal precise monetary or operational effects.

Qualitative analysis helps organizations identify phishing risks, but they utilize this method first to establish a phishing threat as a high-priority vulnerability. Security teams can utilize numerical calculations to determine financial damages stemming from such an assault, including expenses for data retrieval, customer alerts, and regulatory penalties. This organization directs resources toward high-impact risks for more effective mitigation by employing quantitative and qualitative risk assessment methods.

The financial sector demonstrates this combination by having banking institutions simultaneously. Through qualitative analysis, banking institutions identify risks from inside staff and external hackers before categorizing them by risk probability and severity. Using qualitative assessment, organizations employ quantitative analysis to estimate the monetary consequences of previously identified threats.

Qualitative assessment and quantitative analysis help organizations detect their main cybersecurity dangers, but quantitative analysis enables organizations to determine threat consequences and expenses. The redundant methodology helps organizations determine their most dangerous security threats and select the best locations to allocate their cybersecurity budget.

Both risk assessment methods support organizations in creating balanced cybersecurity resource allocation by addressing urgent threats alongside in-depth financial evaluation. Efficient risk reduction regarding cybersecurity posture requires organizations to combine these two approaches in their strategic plan.

## 6.2. Conducting Risk Assessments (ISO 27005, FAIR Model)

Risk assessment forms a crucial foundation for cybersecurity operations because it enables organizations to identify their weaknesses, predict losses they might face, and choose suitable protection methods. Two accepted methods for cybersecurity risk assessment consist of ISO 27005 and the Factor Analysis of Information Risk (FAIR) Model. These cybersecurity frameworks offer organized assessment approaches that combine threat evaluation practices with compliance monitoring and security implementation coordination for strategic business needs.

The International Organization for Standardization developed ISO 27005 as a standardized security risk identification analysis and evaluation method. Multiple industries apply this standard for information security management compliance under ISO 27001 standards. ISO 27005 presents an organized approach that starts by defining risk settings and performs vulnerability detection and probability and impact measurements to execute protection countermeasures. With this method, an organization achieves systematic analysis and security risk control as part of its complete security strategy.

The FAIR Institute developed the FAIR Model, which uses quantitative methods to assess risk according to the organization. FAIR provides financial quantification of risk data because it avoids the subjective classification system used by qualitative risk assessments. The FAIR Model helps organizations by converting risks into measurable elements that include how often losses occur and how large each loss becomes to enable financial-based cyber threat evaluations. Decision-makers gain the ability to deploy resources with maximum efficiency while validating cybersecurity expenditure decisions through this approach.

Figure 6.3.: FAIR Model framework for cyber risk management

ISO 27005 and the FAIR Model offer different assessment methods to analyze risks despite their joint value for the organization. The qualitative and semi-quantitative assessment methods in ISO 27005 allow risk assessment approaches to fit various business situations. ISO 27005 omits a consistent approach to measuring financial risks even though it includes multiple business-environment-suitable risk assessment techniques. The FAIR provides mathematical models that help organizations extend the capabilities of ISO 27005 to evaluate potential losses. When combined, the two models form an all-encompassing framework to handle cybersecurity risk management activities.

The main focus of organizations adopting ISO 27005

consists of defined methods for identifying risks and their treatments. The security management framework classifies risks through specific impact levels that direct the needed security controls. The approach delivers excellent results when upholding compliance requirements and standardizes risk-handling procedures in diverse business areas. Subjectivity within qualitative risk evaluations creates difficulties for organizations in selecting their cybersecurity investments by corresponding actual vulnerability exposure levels.

The FAIR approach enhances risk evaluations through its capability to change security variables into monetary data, enabling better financial risk forecasting. The FAIR methodology allows businesses to calculate security incident probabilities and impact levels, which leads to data-based cybersecurity budget decisions. The methodology enables a better connection between information technology specialists and executive management who use cybersecurity resources to meet corporate objectives.

The models find their practical applications within financial institutions. The international bank employed ISO 27005 to develop its risk management system, which satisfied all regulatory needs. Excessive uncertainty in qualitative risk evaluations forced executives to delay cybersecurity investment decision-making. The bank adopted the FAIR Model to determine the possibility of financial loss from cyber threats, which enabled strategic resource allocation for security purposes.

Figure 6.4.: Risk management process incorporating ISO 27005 and FAIR methodologies

Secure risk assessment benefits from the partnership of ISO 27005 with FAIR. Financial risk assessment capabilities from FAIR analysis enable organizations to use the structured ISO 27005 approach as they better grasp their exposure to risks. Organizations achieve better cybersecurity decision-making by integrating both models because this approach enables them to allocate funding according to precise risk levels.

- Improved risk prioritization by combining structured assessments with financial quantification.

- Enhanced decision-making through data-driven risk analysis, ensuring cybersecurity budgets are allocated effectively.

- Compliance with international security standards while integrating advanced risk modeling techniques.

- Clear communication between security teams and business executives, bridging the gap between technical risk management and financial decision-making.

Organizations' utilization of ISO 27005 and FAIR enables them to create an extensive framework for cybersecurity risk management. Such a dual methodology enables organizations to make qualitative categorization decisions and quantitative risk measurements to make actionable strategic decisions. Businesses can prevent future cyber threats by merging these methodologies to optimize spending on cybersecurity while strengthening their cyber defenses.

## 6.3. Developing an Effective Risk Treatment Plan

Organizations must develop structured risk treatment plans during threat mitigation after finishing risk identification and assessment processes. Management teams of business organizations establish risk treatment frameworks to implement cyber risk management strategies that uphold organization targets and regulatory standards alongside financial and operational limits. Without an orderly plan established by your organization, your cybersecurity exposure will increase, so you will encounter operational disruptions, financial losses, and reputational damage.

Organizations should begin risk treatment plans by creating risk rankings based on projected likelihood and predicted impact levels. The treatment plan for critical risks requiring immediate response expands to long-term solutions for subdued threats which affect essential operations. Risk treatment methods must be implemented according to the cybersecurity framework selected from ISO 27005, the FAIR Model or alternative risk management approaches the organization adopts.

Organizations have four fundamental risk treatment approaches available for their operational needs. They use risk avoidance as their permanent solution to eliminate high-risk operations. Companies that access sensitive customer payment data opt to eliminate payment card storage from their systems by working with secure verification systems that fulfil security protocols. Preventing unsafe actions by avoidance works as an effective solution for dangerous conditions until crucial operational requirements interfere.

Risk reduction involves implementing security controls to minimize the likelihood or impact of cyber threats. This is the most commonly used approach in cybersecurity, as organizations cannot eliminate all risks but can reduce exposure. Measures such as deploying advanced firewalls, enforcing multi-factor authentication, conducting regular security audits, and implementing endpoint detection and response systems are common strategies to reduce cyber risks. By continuously monitoring threats and applying security updates, businesses can limit vulnerabilities and enhance overall resilience.

Organizations protect themselves from cyber threats through security controls, which decrease threat possibilities and worsen their impact. The most frequently used cybersecurity strategy in organizations is because total risk elimination is not feasible, but they can lower their vulnerabilities. Firewalls with enhanced capabilities, authentication policies inc, ident response frameworks, iodic security examinations, and endpoint protection tools represent typical methods organizations use for cyber risk minimization. Businesses achieve resilience by monitoring persistent threats and applying the latest security update releases.

A business distributes its risks through sharing arrangements with external entities. Companies address their security risks through cybersecurity insurance policies that protect them financially during ransomware attacks, data breaches, and regulatory penalties. A business that works with managed security service providers gains access to expert cybersecurity resources while eliminating the need to support personnel within their organization. Organizations lacking specialized cybersecurity staff or needing to save money will find this method useful.

An organization uses risk retention by acknowledging specific risks it accepts because it has limited or unworkable mitigation strategies. Certain cyber threats can remain without immediate response because they appear unlikely to occur or affect business operations only slightly. A company may omit additional security enhancements for isolated legacy systems during their operational existence. The cost-effective nature of risk retention requires continuous monitoring because retained risks must be tracked to prevent their growth. Documenting an effective risk treatment plan requires full details about each risk discovery and matches these with chosen treatment strategies alongside supporting evidence for their selection. The plan establishes defined duties, budgeted resources, and specific timeframes to keep security teams and business stakeholders working together effectively. In order to remain effective, a risk treatment plan needs continuous evaluation for evolving threats and updated requirements.

The application of risk treatment strategies becomes visible through actual cyber incidents. To minimize supply chain threats caused by third-party software usage, a multinational company demanded that vendors maintain stringent cybersecurity requirements for compliance. Supply chain attacks became less probable for the company after conducting third-party security risk assessments and introducing zero-trust design principles as mandatory requirements across the organization.

The financial institution reacted to its ransomware attack by choosing risk reduction through improved backup and disaster recovery protocols. The organization created protected backup systems separate from networks and implemented stronger authentication rules while teaching all workers about cyber threats and their delivery methods. The implemented measures made significant improvements to prevent future disruption occurrences.

A properly executed risk treatment plan must include monitoring systems that track how well vulnerability mitigation solutions work. Organizations must perform routine risk assessments and fake cyber-attack simulations through red team exercises and security event log analysis to track their security enhancements. Security controls maintain relevance through proper tracking while remaining alert to potential risks.

Table 6.1.: Comparison of Cyber Risk Treatment Strategies

| Risk Strategy | Description | Example Use Case | Impact |
|---|---|---|---|
| Risk Avoidance | Eliminating high-risk activities | Removing payment card storage | Reduces attack surface |
| Risk Reduction | Implementing security controls | Deploying firewalls, MFA, security audits | Minimizes exposure to threats |
| Risk Sharing | Transferring risk to third parties | Cyber insurance, outsourced SOC | Reduces financial risk |
| Risk Retention | Accepting low-impact risks | Maintaining legacy systems in isolation | Requires monitoring |

Creating an effective risk treatment plan requires collective work, combining cybersecurity teams with executive leadership and compliance officers. Risk treatment processes should operate dynamically to react to fresh cyber threats that emerge over time. Organizations that continually improve their risk treatment procedures sustain their security strength and reduce the impact of cybersecurity incidents.

# 6.4. Q&A Section

Q: What is the difference between qualitative and quantitative risk assessments?

A: Qualitative uses judgment and scales; quantitative uses data for precise risk evaluation.

Q: How do ISO 27005 and the FAIR Model differ?

A: ISO 27005 is process-based; FAIR quantifies risks in financial terms.

Q: How should organizations develop a risk treatment plan?

A: Identify risks, assess mitigation, set actions, assign roles, and monitor progress.

# 7. Third-Party Risk Management

Most organizations now depend on external vendors, suppliers, and cloud services for production. Business partnerships that attract efficiency and innovation bring substantial cyber risks into organizations. A security breach within third-party system infrastructure exposes data, creating compliance violations and operational disruptions. To effectively handle these risks, businesses must implement a system based on thorough security evaluations that combine real-time monitoring with mandatory adherence to regulatory standards.

This chapter investigates the security dangers vendors, suppliers, and cloud service providers create before delivering methods to evaluate and minimize these security threats. This section presents the best methods for assessing third-party security while providing examples of frameworks like Service Organization Control 2, Standardized Information Gathering, and Cloud Security Alliance Security, Trust, and Assurance Registry. Organizations implementing strong risk management programs diminish their attack-exposed areas while protecting sensitive data and meeting all necessary regulations.

# 7.1. Risks from Vendors, Suppliers, and Cloud Service Providers

Modern business operations benefit extensively from third-party entities because these entities help organizations grow their capabilities and achieve technological integration while lowering costs. Using vendors and suppliers alongside cloud service providers leads to security vulnerabilities that endanger data authenticity and regulatory rules and erode entire endpoint security structures. Cyber attackers exploit weaknesses in third-party ecosystems by focusing attacks on inadequate security measures, compromised passwords, and unsecured systems to achieve illicit access.

Organizations face substantial security threats whenever third parties obtain unauthorized system access to their sensitive information. When vendors need privileged access for their work activities, security breaches become possible because weak authentication methods or over-excessive privileges create security vulnerabilities. The attackers exploit compromised vendor credentials to exploratively navigate through organizational networks while abducting sensitive information and causing operational interference.

Adopting supply chain attacks remains a vital security concern since attackers exploit weak points in software updates, hardware components, or managed services to inject harmful code into trusted systems. The attacks are dangerous because they leverage a supplier's trusted role to carry malware without detection. The SolarWinds attack showed that malicious updates to the SolarWinds system disrupted operations at many government agencies and multinational businesses across thousands of affected organizations.

Cloud service providers create new security risks when their customers share infrastructure and make mistakes in configuration while depending on third-party security services. Organizations need to protect their cloud applications and configurations under the shared responsibility model, but the provider must secure the fundamental infrastructure. Inadequate cloud security implementation among organizations causes their sensitive information to surface because of incorrect data storage setups, exposed databases, and deficient access control management methods.

When third parties fail to secure systems properly, the consequences will lead to substantial regulatory penalties. Organizations must follow data protection laws such as the General Data Protection Regulation, the Health Insurance Portability and Accountability Act, and the Payment Card Industry Data Security Standard when their vendors process sensitive data. Security breaches in third-party infrastructure platforms lead to financial penalties, operational interruptions, and company reputation damage.

Security incidents affecting vendors result in both financial and operational business risks. The origin of a data breach from vendor services leads organizations to face increased downtime and financial costs from legal suits, together with extensive losses of customer trust. Reliable services and continued operations become jeopardized when cyberattacks target manufacturing or logistics partners within supply chains.

Table 7.1.: Common Third-Party Cyber Risks and Mitigation Strategies

| Risk Type | Description | Mitigation Strategies |
|---|---|---|
| Unauthorized Access | Risk of credential compromise. | Enforce least privilege, multi-factor authentication, monitor access. |
| Supply Chain Attacks | Malicious code via compromised software or hardware. | Regular security assessments, integrity checks, and secure development. |
| Data Breaches | Weak security exposes sensitive data. | Use encryption, secure sharing, and conduct regular audits. |
| Cloud Misconfigurations | Misconfigurations expose data and increase risks. | Automated security tools, enforce identity controls, and audit regularly. |
| Compliance Violations | Vendors must meet regulatory requirements. | Require certifications (SOC 2, ISO 27001, GDPR compliance). |

Organizations must develop a systematic vendor risk management system that handles these security challenges. All vendors must perform the initial phase of security assessments during their onboarding process to verify their compliance with cybersecurity security standards. Security assessments should evaluate third parties' security policies, access control systems, and ability to respond to incidents.

Creating vendor risk tiers enables organizations to organize their suppliers according to their system access to critical resources and their exposure to sensitive information. Security requirements for vendors who handle critical assets such as cloud services and payment transactions need strict controls with ongoing monitoring procedures over basic supplier security measures.

Organizations greatly reduce third-party risks by implementing binding security obligations in their contracts. Businesses need to insert cybersecurity terms into their supplier contracts, which define their security requirements, data defense protocols, and legal reporting duties in case of breaches. The service level agreements must set up responsibility lists for security incidents with clear requirements to comply with existing security frameworks.

Organizations must establish ongoing vendor security posture surveillance to find new threats. They benefit from using risk management platforms for vendor security tracking, which enables both breach monitoring and compliance evaluation. Organizations use automated tools to see third-party security risks live so they can act ahead to stop incidents from worsening.

By purchasing cyber insurance, organizations can protect themselves from the financial consequences of vendor-caused breaches. Organizations secure third-party risk insurance, which provides two primary coverage elements for supply chain security and vendor compliance incidents. The financial protection offered by insurance is a supplemental measure to complement robust security systems, although it does not substitute essential security measures.

Organizations must develop incident response plans combining third-party entities to improve their risk management efforts. Security measures must integrate vendors in cybersecurity response plans to guarantee joint efforts between organizations during cyber breaches. Fast incident response and reduced downtime become possible as security teams use well-defined communication pathways with suppliers.

Businesses' dependency on third-party providers has driven threat development toward advanced assault methods that target vendor delivery networks. Organizations that implement proactive third-party risk management practices can help their vendors, suppliers, and cloud providers develop robust security systems, which results in lower chances of supply chain attacks and data breaches.

## 7.2. Best Practices for Third-Party Security Assessments

Organizations need to assess the current security position of their third-party vendors to determine their permission level for sensitive systems or data access. Without sufficient assessment, organizations face increased risks of supply chain attacks and data breaches and fail to comply with regulatory requirements. A properly organized third-party security evaluation reduces these vulnerabilities by verifying security best practices and fulfilling vendor compliance requirements.

Vendor security assessments include security audits and strict security questionnaires, which vendors must complete. Security evaluations must also include inspection of authentication methods, encryption protocols, permission systems, and incident response plans. Organizations use vendor responses to detect possible vulnerabilities that may exist prior to integrating their third-party services.

Third-party system vulnerability detection depends on penetration testing and automated vulnerability scanning methods. Through ethical hacking methods and automated scans, organizations reveal the types of misconfigurations, dated software, and many exploitable weaknesses that attackers would use. Periodic assessment sessions must happen to guarantee that vendors preserve robust security safeguards from start to finish their tasks.

An organization must continuously track vendor security status to spot security incidents, compliance issues, and emerging threats. Organizations must use real-time automated tracking solutions to monitor their vendor security positions. Organizations gain access to threat intelligence feeds and security monitoring platforms to spot third-party system vulnerabilities or breaches that trigger immediate responses.

Vendor security assessments fundamentally require the implementation of tight access control systems. The assigned access should never exceed what vendors need to execute their work assignments successfully. Security systems implemented through access control measures that combine multiple authentication methods reduce unauthorized entry points while protecting against security risks.

Organizations must establish contractual security requirements that vendors follow cybersecurity standards. Service agreements must contain security obligations, such as requirements to protect data, notify about breaches, and adhere to applicable industrial regulations. Vendor contracts should include explicit definitions of security expectations, which creates legal methods to handle security incidents and establishes vendor accountability.

The secure maintenance of vendor-affiliated services depends on periodic reviews to validate compliance with standards. Management must regularly check vendor security controls to ensure they meet established security policies. Security assessments of third-party systems need ongoing updates to track emerging threats and evolving regulatory demands.

Organizations implementing structured security assessments, continuous monitoring, strict access control policies, and clear contractual obligations will decrease third-party risks while developing a robust cybersecurity system. Organizations focusing on vendor security proactively will stop external security threats against their supply chain and data leakages while maintaining continuous compliance, resulting in sustained business operations.

# 7.3. How to Enforce Compliance with SOC 2, SIG, and CSA STAR

Compliance frameworks can develop standards security controls and verify that third-party vendors fulfill their cybersecurity requirements. The three most commonly utilized frameworks for verifying third-party security assurance include Service Organization Control 2, Standardized Information Gathering, and the Cloud Security Alliance Security Trust and Assurance Registry.

Service Organization Control 2 utilizes five trust service criteria to evaluate security, availability, processing integrity, confidentiality, and privacy. The implementation procedures require vendors to establish robust security measures that safeguard customer information. Organizations that care for sensitive information with their vendor networks must ask for Service Organization Control 2 reports to show compliance.

Standardized Information Gathering is a common security questionnaire that assesses the security position of external business partners. This assessment method establishes a logical process for inspecting vendor security through domains that showcase network safety, ID administration, data protection, and incident responses.

The Cloud Security Alliance Security Trust and Assurance Registry caters especially to cloud service providers. The model enables certification activities that examine cloud practices for security best practices alongside international security standards. Organizations must verify that cloud vendors maintain their Cloud Security Alliance Security, Trust, and Assurance Registry certification to confirm their security expectations.

Organizations demonstrate better security while minimizing supply chain attacks through standard vendor risk assessments enabled by compliance framework implementation.

# 7.4. Q&A Section

Q: What is the significance of third-party risk management?

A: Vendors access data, making them cyberattack targets, leading to breaches and penalties.

Q: What risks do most cloud service providers present?

A: Misconfigurations, insecure APIs, privilege abuse, and lack of visibility.

Q: Businesses need what methods to track vendor security performance?

A: Automated systems and regular assessments detect risks and ensure compliance.

Q: What security terms should vendor contracts include?

A: Access controls, encryption, breach reporting, compliance rules, and security checks.

Q: Compliance frameworks provide what type of assistance?

A: They set security standards, reducing risks and ensuring best practices.

# 8. Incident Response and Crisis Management

Business organizations must maintain established processes that efficiently address unavoidable cyber threats. This chapter covers the development process for incident response plans, along with an overview of crucial crisis management roles and testing methods for response plans. The study presents two contrasting examples of response activities demonstrating preparedness results versus unpreparedness leading to negative outcomes. The final part addresses frequently asked questions regarding incident response plans and crisis management.

## 8.1. Developing an Incident Response Plan (IRP)

Incident response plans offer a methodical way to discover, restrict, manage, and restore cyber threats. Implementing a carefully organized plan helps organizations minimize both system downtime and financial costs, preserve their reputation, and maintain regulatory compliance. Organizations that fail to develop response strategies will witness disorganized responses int, intensified enemy penetration, and longer duration of recovery processes.

Developing an effective incident response plan uses organized phases for successfully managing cyber threats.

- **Preparation:** Organizations must assess potential threats, establish detection mechanisms, and train response teams to ensure a swift reaction to cyber incidents.

- **Detection and Analysis:** Once an incident is identified, security teams assess the nature and severity of the attack, gathering intelligence to determine the best response strategy.

- **Containment:** Immediate measures are taken to isolate affected systems and prevent the threat from spreading across the network.

- **Eradication:** Malicious components are removed, and security vulnerabilities exploited in the attack are patched to prevent reinfection.

- **Recovery:** Systems are restored to normal operations, ensuring the business resumes activities securely and without residual risks.

- **Lessons Learned:** The incident is reviewed, response actions are analyzed, and the plan is refined to improve future handling of similar threats.

An effective response plan requires preparation as its fundamental base. Organizations should take a proactive approach by analyzing their risk environment and detecting potential attack routes while deploying advanced security defense systems. Response team members receive appropriate training, which enables them to perform incident management tasks successfully. Any detailed response plan will experience failure during execution when there is no preparation in place.

Analysis and detection function as vital elements that help reduce the extent of damages. Security operators need to determine promptly which system has been targeted and how serious this attack is to the entire network. When organizations identify incidents early, they can launch containment measures accompanied by mitigation responses quickly.

An effective containment strategy stops the ongoing attack from worsening its effects. For different types of attacks, containment measures can include disconnecting impacted hardware, using network blackout protocols, and partitioning compromised systems. Successful containment procedures restrict the spreading of attacks while enabling a more extensive study of the incident.

The fundamental root of the attack requires complete elimination according to eradication procedures. The phase relies on three essential measures: destroying malware, repairing vulnerable areas, and terminating compromised access credentials so the attack cannot remain active in the environment. Operations recovery focuses on two main objectives: system restoration and normal operation resumption while managing the organization's safety against new security threats. Securely backed-up systems and disaster recovery procedures provide controlled pathways for complete system recovery.

An incident response plan requires a post-incident review as its concluding stage. Because of lessons learned from each incident, security policies enhance their effectiveness, and organizations improve detection capabilities while developing better response strategies. Organizations that skip this step will remain blind to their repeated security weaknesses, which endangers their systems to continued cyberattacks.

Routine evaluations and plan upkeep are fundamental for maintaining the effectiveness of business responses against threats since threat methods continue to change. Failure to review plans results in unproductive responses to threats, using strategies that fail to protect against contemporary attack methods. Companies that update their response protocols regularly will stay protected from developing cyber threats.

# 8.2. Key Roles in Cyber Crisis Management

Effective incident response demands technical competence and team coordination of specific organizational units due to their separate responsibilities. The incident response team members handle threat analysis and risk reduction while implementing the containment approach. Crisis managers oversee the entire process to maintain effective communication and decision-making activities. The organization's legal team ensures regulatory adherence alongside liability reduction, and public relations personnel handle communications to defend the company's reputation. Executive leaders create successful incident responses by ensuring the achievement of organizational goals and properly distributing required resources.

The teams must establish precise communication pathways to help prevent response delays and confusion in a crisis. A chaotic reaction can lead to extended drops in service, financial sanctions, and diminished stakeholder credibility.

## 8.3. How to Test and Improve Response Plans

A response plan gains strength from successful execution during actual cyber incidents. Organizations that fail to regularly test and refine their plans will be unprepared for real cyber attacks. Several testing methods and improvement strategies must be implemented to make incident response plans effective.

The essential testing approach includes holding tabletop drills that create simulated security situations within controlled environments. Team response exercises enable personnel to review circumstances while discussing their movements and spotting cooperation and decision-making weaknesses. Organization scenarios enable detailed evaluation, which helps teams amend their response plans while strengthening their internal communication methods.

Security professionals who serve as attackers perform red team assessments to evaluate the defensive measures of organizations. Such practical simulations help organizations uncover security risks that attackers could potentially abuse. Organizations can focus their response capability upgrades on system weaknesses by understanding operational weaknesses.

- **Tabletop Exercises:** These are structured discussions where teams analyze hypothetical cyber incidents and evaluate response strategies in a controlled setting.

- **Red Team Assessments:** Security professionals simulate real-world attacks to test the organization's detection and defence capabilities.

- **Live Drills:** Response teams participate in full-scale simulations to measure their ability to detect, contain, and mitigate active threats.

- **Employee Training:** Staff members are educated on recognizing cyber threats, adhering to security protocols, and responding appropriately to incidents.

- **Performance Metrics:** Key indicators such as response time, containment effectiveness, and recovery speed help measure the overall efficiency of the response plan.

Organizations can achieve the highest test of preparedness by conducting live drills. The difference between tabletop exercises and these drills consists of real-time simulations assessing response teams' abilities to identify threats, stop their spread, and minimize the damage. The execution of live drills shows organizational weaknesses, which makes it possible to identify urgent areas for improvement.

Implementing employee training is a fundamental factor that strengthens an organization's cybersecurity defenses. The primary reason behind security breaches stems from human mistakes, so workers need training in identifying phishing techniques, correctly using security protocols, and responding quickly to unusual activities. Organizations that train their staff members properly use them as their primary defense system against cyber attacks.

A resilient cybersecurity strategy requires ongoing testing and continuous improvements as its foundation for success. The synergy between simulations, real-world attack testing, staff training, and performance analysis enables organizations to handle cyber incidents efficiently. Organizations that test their response plans before emergencies will be better prepared to decrease attack impacts while quickly returning to standard operations after incidents.

## 8.4. Case Study: Effective vs. Failed Incident Response Strategies

Incident response strategies determine whether organizations will bounce back quickly or experience complete failure. Reality-based scenarios demonstrate that prepared organizations limit their losses through robust incident response plans, while unprepared organizations face major setbacks.

A multinational financial institution displayed successful incident response actions when its state-of-the-art ransomware attack occurred. Attackers encrypted vital operational data, which they requested payment to decrypt. Security teams immediately detected the breach by employing proactive threat detection and their practised response framework. The team reacted swiftly to cut off the affected systems, thus stopping the malware from spreading laterally. Because of its robust data backup system, the organization can reset its default settings directly without payment from the attackers. The organization activated communication systems immediately to notify internal departments and external partners and maintain operational ongoing status. Operations restarted quickly, and financial disruption remained minor while customers kept their faith in the organization's management.

The major hospital network faced a comparable attack yet did not possess an organized response plan during the incident. Ransomware infected all interconnected patient systems that encrypted medical appointment data and patient records while seizing control of hospital equipment. The lack of proper preparation forced the IT team to fight unsuccessfully against the attack and did not keep recent backups. Patient care experienced delays, while the hospital maintained only manual functions because of the attack. Not having a strategic communication approach led hospital personnel and patients to stay in the dark, thus causing increased worry and disarray. Lack of public confidence led to major challenges for the organization because it failed to safeguard important medical data, triggering legal and regulatory investigations. The financial consequences exceeded the ransom payment when combined with regulatory penalties, the harm caused to the hospital's reputation, and long periods of operational disruption.

These incidents demonstrate which elements determine whether incident response plans succeed or fail. Organizations that maintain early detection capabilities, containment protocols, recovery plans, and clear communication systems reduce the impact of cyber incidents. Businesses without incident preparation will suffer from extended outages, monetary losses, and enduring negative impacts on their brands. Organizations must implement proper cybersecurity measures to protect themselves from inevitable threats because strategic planning ensures they can stay resilient against changing threats.

# 8.5. Q&A Section

Q: What is the main distinction between incident response and crisis management?

A: The main distinction between incident response and crisis management rests in how each handles the cyber situation. Protection of a cyber incident through incident response occurs by identifying incidents followed by preventing their expansion and minimizing their impact. The crisis management process handles problems that span through financial domains and reputation management along with legal elements.

Q: How often should incident response plans undergo updates?

A: The incident response plan requires yearly assessment and update whenever infrastructure adjusts or when new regulatory needs emerge or when new cyber threats appear.

Q: What essential elements enable an effective response team?

A: The formation of an effective response team depends on cybersecurity specialists together with crisis managers in addition to legal advisors and public relations professionals along with executives for ensuring complete coordinated solutions.

Q: Why is maintaining proper communication essential during a cyber incident?

A: Communicating with accuracy at the right time lets internal staff members and customers and regulatory agencies stay informed while decreasing false information and keeping confidence levels high.

Q: Detection of a cyber attack leads to immediate action according to which step?

A: The initial priority for a cyber incident remains recorded as containment because responders need to cut off affected systems from network access in order to analyze the situation.

Q: What steps should organizations follow regarding response time management?

A: Organizations which combine automatic threat detection with continuous staff development alongside established response plans become able to respond immediately and reduce cyber-attack consequences.

# Part III.

# Compliance : Meeting Regulatory and Industry Standards

# 9. Understanding Cybersecurity Compliance

Digital businesses need cybersecurity compliance as an essential operating requirement within the digital environment. The industry requirement encompasses following regulations, frameworks, and best practices that protect data and systems and ensure operational stability. The foundation built by compliance standards allows organizations to protect their security base but should not negate active threat prevention. The chapter investigates the differences between compliance and security along with regulatory advantages and provides a general overview of worldwide compliance requirements.

## 9.1. Compliance vs. Security: Key Differences

The goals of compliance and security are related concepts with separate functions. The term compliance implies adherence to particular regulations alongside industry standards and legal demands that governing bodies set as requirements. The practice of security requires businesses to consistently deploy protective defenses to fight different kinds of cyber attacks.

Stand-alone compliance does not protect a company from cyber attacks because threat monitoring and defense system updates remain essential for preventing infections. Businesses focus on documented policies and conduct periodic assessments to fulfil compliance requirements derived from audit demands. Security exists as a practice that requires organizations to regularly update their defense strategies against changing security risks over time.

An organization that follows the Payment Card Industry Data Security Standard (PCI DSS) requirements through credit card data encryption remains at risk of suffering damage via a data breach due to deficient incident response planning practices. Businesses dedicated only to compliance standards establish structured security procedures, yet they might neglect emerging security dangers.

# 9.2. Benefits of Cybersecurity Compliance for Businesses

Organizations receive extensive advantages from cybersecurity compliance standards beyond basic regulatory needs. Organizational compliance investments create higher safety profiles alongside better stakeholder trust and reduced financial damages and operational risks due to cyber threats.

The principal advantage of compliance implementation is better risk control. By implementing security policies and best practices, organizations lower security breaches and exposure. Firms that implement compliance frameworks stay protected from significant operational setbacks that result from security failures. Compliance creates better accountability through its ability to communicate the security responsibilities entrusted to employees and stakeholders in maintaining cybersecurity.

Both security and compliance function as an enhancer of business credibility while building increased customer trust. Organizations can win more consumer business with the trust of their business partners through their displayed dedication to data protection practices. Certifications such as ISO 27001, SOC 2, or PCI DSS are industry-recognized proof of robust security measures. Organizations operating in finance and healthcare sectors that maintain compliance standards achieve substantial competitive advantages.

Following regulatory guidelines provides defense against both legal consequences and financial damages to businesses. Several frameworks impose substantial fines for non-compliance, including:

- *General Data Protection Regulation (GDPR):* Non-compliance can lead to fines of up to 4% of global annual revenue or €20 million, whichever is higher.

- *California Consumer Privacy Act (CCPA):* Violations can result in penalties of up to $7,500 per incident for intentional breaches.

- *Health Insurance Portability and Accountability Act (HIPAA):* Non-compliance penalties can range from thousands to millions of dollars, depending on the severity of the violation.

- *Payment Card Industry Data Security Standard (PCI DSS):* Non-compliant businesses risk increased transaction fees, lawsuits, or the loss of their ability to process payments.

The primary importance of compliance in incident response must be better recognized in cybersecurity strategies. Detailed response plans represent a regulatory requirement that businesses must prepare under many different compliance regimes to swiftly discover cyber threats and stop and restore operations. Businesses operating without prepared measures face increased periods of system unavailability alongside greater financial losses and negative reputation consequences during security incidents.

Organizations must maintain compliance as an operational approach instead of treating it as a mandatory requirement. Organizations that unite compliance standards with proactive cybersecurity measures will protect their business data, operational tasks, and company reputation from cyber risk threats.

# 9.3. Overview of Global Compliance Mandates

The management of risks through cybersecurity compliance involves following rules designed to secure confidential organizational data. Modern threats and their evolving nature prompt compliance frameworks to deliver organized instructions about security control deployment, risk control, and legal responsibilities fulfillment. Different industries and jurisdictions maintain separate requirements that organizations need to follow as part of their compliance practice. This part investigates major global cybersecurity regulations together with their required applications.

## General Data Protection Regulation (GDPR)

Under the General Data Protection Regulation (GDPR), European Union individuals gain the strongest data protection enforcement through laws determining how organizations handle the personal data they process from EU residents. Organizations dealing with data from any EU citizen must follow the GDPR no matter where their operations are based. The GDPR implements mandatory guidelines about data transparency in combination with user consent frameworks and security standards for personal data protection.

GDPR implements a significant requirement through the right to be forgotten, which enables individuals to demand the removal of their personal information. To comply with GDPR requirements, organizations must use encryption, perform recurrent risk assessments, and report all detected breaches to authorities within 72 hours. Fines for non-compliance with GDPR can reach a maximum of four percent of total annual global revenue or twenty million euros, depending on which amount exceeds the other.

The technology giant received a one-billion-euro enforcement penalty from GDPR authorities after breaking regulations about data movement between American and European Union territories. This incident demonstrates why organizations must protect data that crosses borders and fulfill difficult regulatory requirements.

## Health Insurance Portability and Accountability Act (HIPAA)

HIPAA serves as a federal standard to create security protocols which safeguard personal health information during processing by healthcare organizations and their medical record processor business partners. The healthcare organization needs to create different systems for medical data protection through administrative practices and physical controls with technical protection technologies.

Under the HIPAA Security Rule healthcare organizations must implement encryption requirements to protect electronic health information along with restricted access systems while conducting continuous information system monitoring. Healthcare facilities need to perform continuous risk assessment operations which help them find security weaknesses in their data protection systems. All healthcare organizations that fail to comply with HIPAA rules risk extreme financial and legal consequences as well as possible criminal prosecution.

The exposure of millions of patient medical files resulted from the non-compliance of a major medical service provider. The healthcare sector requires robust compliance frameworks due to the organization receiving major penalties and legal sanctions from its insufficient security measures.

## Payment Card Industry Data Security Standard (PCI DSS)

Payment card handling agencies must adhere to the Payment Card Industry Data Security Standard (PCI DSS) established worldwide to defend transaction data from fraud and protect privacy. Every organization dealign with payment data or cardholder personal records needs to fulfill the requirements set by this standard. The standard contains twelve compulsory security criteria which include both encryption alongside access control systems along with network partitioning methods and periodic security assessment programs.

The protection of payment data must be ensured by organizations through security policies to keep PCI DSS compliance. The penalties imposed on non-compliant businesses include payment card network restrictions and both legal liability and monetary penalties.

## ISO/IEC 27001: Information Security Management System

The ISO/IEC 27001 standard provides a structured approach for establishing, maintaining, and improving an information security management system. Unlike regulatory mandates that impose specific security measures, ISO 27001 focuses on risk-based security practices that organizations can tailor to their operational needs.

Many enterprises seek ISO 27001 certification to demonstrate compliance with best practices, enhance security governance, and strengthen customer trust. The standard covers various aspects of cybersecurity, including risk assessment, continuous monitoring, security awareness training, and incident response planning.

Global technology companies and cloud service providers have adopted ISO 27001 to ensure compliance with international security standards. Achieving certification not only enhances credibility but also helps organizations align their cybersecurity strategies with regulatory requirements.

## Cybersecurity Maturity Model Certification (CMMC)

The Cybersecurity Maturity Model Certification (CMMC) is a framework developed by the United States Department of Defense to strengthen the security of the defense industrial base. It establishes five maturity levels that contractors must achieve to handle controlled unclassified information.

Unlike other compliance mandates, CMMC requires independent third-party assessments to verify that organizations meet cybersecurity requirements. Contractors failing to obtain the required certification may be ineligible for government contracts.

A cybersecurity breach in the defense sector occurred when a contractor handling classified naval data experienced a cyberattack that resulted in the theft of sensitive military information. This incident reinforced the necessity of CMMC compliance in safeguarding national security assets.

# California Consumer Privacy Act (CCPA)

The California Consumer Privacy Act (CCPA) is a data protection law that grants California residents rights over their personal information. Businesses subject to CCPA must disclose data collection practices, provide consumers with opt-out mechanisms, and ensure transparency in data sharing.

While similar to GDPR, CCPA primarily applies to for-profit organizations meeting certain revenue and data processing thresholds. Non-compliance can result in regulatory penalties and consumer lawsuits.

A significant enforcement case under CCPA involved a major online retailer fined for failing to inform customers about data sharing practices. The case underscored the growing importance of data privacy laws in the United States and the necessity for organizations to implement comprehensive compliance programs.

## National Institute of Standards and Technology (NIST) Cybersecurity Framework

The NIST Cybersecurity Framework is a widely adopted set of guidelines designed to help organizations manage cybersecurity risks. It provides a flexible, risk-based approach to security governance, structured around five core functions: identify, protect, detect, respond, and recover.

Federal agencies and private sector organizations utilize the NIST framework as a best-practice model for strengthening cybersecurity defenses. The framework is particularly beneficial for organizations that require standardized risk management methodologies.

For instance, financial institutions and critical infrastructure providers leverage NIST guidelines to enhance their security postures and comply with regulatory requirements. The adoption of the framework helps organizations establish resilient cybersecurity programs that align with industry standards.

# 9.4. The Evolving Cybersecurity Compliance Landscape

The cybersecurity compliance domain evolves through the introduction of new security threats combined with regulatory modifications. Security practices adopted by organizations with operations in multiple jurisdictions need to merge with various regulatory requirements to achieve both legal and operational stability.

Basic compliance with regulations does not provide security protection to businesses because they must address contemporary cyber threats above regulatory baseline requirements.

Cybersecurity compliance faces its main challenge because multiple regulations intersect with each other. The Garcia Corporation operating throughout multiple jurisdictions must meet GDPR standards to protect European data along with PCI DSS requirements for payment security and HIPAA standards for U.S. healthcare. Businesses face auditing complexity and operational expenses and security gaps when they work with multiple security framework standards. Businesses tackle this issue through comprehensive risk management solutions which establish one framework for integrating various security requirements.

The intensification of regulatory enforcement resulted from major cyber incidents occurring worldwide. Security experts discovered that the SolarWinds supply chain attack demonstrated serious flaws in security models grounded in compliance standards. Various organizations achieved technical compliance while these organizations had weak supply chain monitoring systems in place. The introduction of more detailed standards through CISA and ENISA requires agencies to focus on immediate threat detection together with enhanced third-party risk handling.

A structured approach to compliance includes:

- *Risk-Based Compliance:* Organizations should assess their unique risk landscape instead of merely following regulatory checklists.

- *Continuous Monitoring:* Real-time threat detection and automated compliance assessments improve security posture.

- *Security Beyond Compliance:* Advanced security measures such as AI-driven anomaly detection, zero-trust models, and endpoint protection complement regulatory adherence.

- *Incident Readiness:* Regular security drills, penetration testing, and crisis management planning enhance resilience.

- *Global Standardization:* Many businesses are adopting ISO 27001 and NIST frameworks to maintain consistency across different regulatory environments.

The finance industry together with healthcare proves by example that compliance maintains its relationship with proactive security measures. AITechnology-based fraud detection systems allow financial institutions to meet their AML expectations while building improved systems to identify present threats in real time. Medical facilities defend themselves against ransomware through zero-trust security systems which link to ongoing HIPAA requirement compliance by implementing biometric authentication.

Strategic compliance methods of the future will use automated systems that merge with artificial intelligence risk assessment methods anchored by global regulatory standards. Security-based compliance development by organizations leads to superior protection from current and future threats while creating durable systems.

# 9.5. Q&A Section

Q: Which factors make compliance insufficient to achieve cybersecurity?

A: By definition compliance defines fundamental security requirements yet fails to counter present-time security threats.By definition compliance defines fundamental security requirements yet fails to counter present-time security threats. The requirements of compliance do not encompass every cybersecurity aspect as organizations must continuously monitor systems and proactively mitigate threats through risk assessments for effective protection.

Q: Businesses must perform compliance audits. What frequency rate should they follow?

A: Businesses and highly regulated industries need to conduct audits at least once per year and must schedule additional audits when changes occur in their systems.

Q: What consequences do businesses that fail to comply face?

A: Penalties vary by regulation. Companies that violate GDPR requirements will face a maximum penalty of 4 per cent of their worldwide revenue profits. Violation of HIPAA and PCI DSS standards creates risks for business operations or financial consequences, along with potential legal actions.

Q: Small businesses need to know which budget size and approach will help them maintain compliance standards.

A: Small enterprises can execute basic security measures through encryption software, staff training programs, and multi-factor authentication systems. Organizations can use exterior security auditing services with cloud security systems to lower security costs without compromising regulatory requirements.

Q: Are compliance requirements the same across industries?

A: Compliance requirements differ depending on your sector and geographic region. Different healthcare organizations must follow HIPAA regulations, while financial institutions need to uphold PCI DSS standards. Companies operating in Europe also need to judge GDPR rules.

Q: How well a company follows established compliance standards affects cybersecurity insurance premiums?

A: Insurers normally need businesses to demonstrate compliance standards for insurance coverage. Organizations demonstrating cybersecurity commitment through compliance achieve reduced premiums and better insurance policy conditions.

Q: What stands as the main obstacle for organizations when they attempt to sustain compliance?

A: Several organizations face difficulties maintaining compliance as they need to adapt security controls to new regulations and compliance requirements. Organizations must also update their policies frequently while training staff and monitoring regulatory modifications.

# 10. Regulatory Standards and Compliance-Driven Security Programs

Organizations need to follow Cybersecurity compliance as their central component for modern risk management to fulfill their legal and regulatory and industry-specific security standards. Compliance frameworks structure guidelines to secure sensitive data while reducing risks and showing evidence of security duties. Accomplishing compliance standards fails to serve as an adequate security guarantee. Broad cybersecurity strategies require organizations to embed compliance requirements so they can develop security programs which resist threats while adapting to new dangers.

This section discusses essential regulatory standards and demonstrates how compliance connects with security controls and describes compliance obstacles while outlining best practices for a security framework based on compliance principles. The text explores how Compliance as a Service (CaaS) functions and automation in Governance Risk and Compliance (GRC) and demonstrates effective ways to measure compliance success.

# 10.1. Understanding Key Compliance Frameworks

Regulatory standards and compliance frameworks establish fundamental security requirements for organizations across different industries and jurisdictions. Each framework provides structured guidelines for protecting data, managing risks, and ensuring operational security. However, compliance obligations vary depending on the industry, geographic location, and regulatory authority. Identifying and aligning with the relevant frameworks is essential for achieving compliance and strengthening security posture.

- ISO 27001: A globally recognized standard for information security management systems (ISMS). It defines a systematic approach to securing sensitive information through risk management, security policies, and procedural controls. ISO 27001 certification demonstrates an organization's commitment to maintaining robust cybersecurity measures.

- NIST 800-53: A comprehensive framework developed by the U.S. National Institute of Standards and Technology (NIST). It provides detailed security and privacy controls for federal agencies and contractors handling government data, ensuring protection against cyber threats, unauthorized access, and data breaches.

- Sarbanes-Oxley Act (SOX): A U.S. regulation designed to enforce stringent financial reporting controls. Publicly traded companies must implement security measures that protect the integrity and confidentiality of financial data, preventing fraud and ensuring compliance with auditing requirements.

- Health Insurance Portability and Accountability Act (HIPAA): A regulatory standard governing the confidentiality, integrity, and availability of patient health information (PHI) in the U.S. It mandates strict access controls, data encryption, and audit logs to safeguard sensitive medical records from unauthorized exposure.

- General Data Protection Regulation (GDPR): The European Union's data protection law that regulates the collection, processing, and storage of personal data. GDPR emphasizes user rights, data minimization, breach notification requirements, and imposes substantial financial penalties for non-compliance.

- Payment Card Industry Data Security Standard (PCI DSS): A mandatory security framework for businesses handling payment card transactions. It enforces encryption, authentication, and network security controls to protect cardholder data and prevent financial fraud.

- System and Organization Controls 2 (SOC 2): A compliance standard designed for technology service providers, emphasizing security, availability, processing integrity, confidentiality, and privacy. SOC 2 audits assess an organization's adherence to trust principles in cloud computing, data processing, and outsourced IT services.

Each of these frameworks is tailored to mitigate risks associated with cyber threats, data breaches, and compliance violations. However, achieving compliance alone does not equate to comprehensive security. Organizations must operationalize security controls, conduct continuous risk assessments, and integrate compliance within their cybersecurity strategies to ensure long-term resilience against evolving cyber threats.

## 10.2. Mapping Compliance Requirements to Security Controls

Regulatory mandates establish security objectives, but they do not provide explicit technical guidance on implementation. Organizations must translate compliance requirements into enforceable security measures to achieve both regulatory adherence and robust cybersecurity.

- Identity and Access Management (IAM): Regulations such as HIPAA, PCI DSS, and ISO 27001 mandate strong authentication mechanisms, including multi-factor authentication (MFA) and role-based access control (RBAC). These measures ensure that only authorized personnel access sensitive systems and data, minimizing insider threats and unauthorized access.

- Data Encryption: Compliance frameworks such as GDPR and PCI DSS require organizations to implement encryption for sensitive data both at rest and in transit. Strong encryption protocols, such as AES-256 and TLS, prevent data exposure in case of breaches, unauthorized interception, or data theft.

- Threat Detection and Incident Response: Standards like NIST 800-53 and ISO 27001 emphasize the importance of real-time security monitoring, anomaly detection, and automated incident response. Security Information and Event Management (SIEM) solutions, intrusion detection systems (IDS), and automated log analysis help organizations detect, investigate, and contain threats efficiently.

- Risk Assessments and Auditing: SOC 2, GDPR, and ISO 27001 require organizations to conduct periodic security audits and risk assessments. These assessments help identify vulnerabilities, evaluate security control effectiveness, and ensure continuous compliance with evolving regulatory standards.

- Secure Software Development: Compliance frameworks such as PCI DSS and NIST 800-53 enforce secure coding practices, static and dynamic vulnerability scanning, and secure software development lifecycle (SDLC) practices. Regular code reviews, penetration testing, and DevSecOps integration reduce software-related security risks.

Aligning security controls with compliance objectives strengthens an organization's overall security posture while ensuring regulatory adherence. A proactive compliance strategy integrates security best practices with continuous monitoring, risk assessment, and incident response to mitigate both regulatory and cyber threats effectively.

## 10.3. Common Compliance Pitfalls and How to Avoid Them

Achieving and maintaining cybersecurity compliance is a complex process that requires more than just meeting regulatory requirements. Many organizations struggle with compliance due to poor planning, insufficient resources, and an over-reliance on checklist-based approaches. Compliance failures not only lead to regulatory penalties but also expose organizations to significant security risks. Addressing common pitfalls through proactive strategies ensures a more resilient compliance program.

- Treating compliance as a one-time achievement: Compliance is an ongoing process that requires continuous monitoring, regular policy updates, and periodic risk assessments. Organizations must establish mechanisms for tracking regulatory changes and adapting security measures accordingly.

- Isolating compliance from broader security strategies: Compliance should be seamlessly integrated into cybersecurity frameworks rather than treated as an independent function. A unified approach ensures that security policies, incident response protocols, and risk management strategies align with regulatory mandates.

- Ignoring third-party risks: Many organizations fail to assess the security and compliance status of third-party vendors and service providers. Supply chain vulnerabilities pose significant risks, making it essential to conduct thorough vendor risk assessments and enforce compliance requirements through contractual obligations.

- Poor documentation and audit readiness: Regulatory audits demand well-documented security policies, access controls, and incident response records. Organizations that lack comprehensive documentation may struggle to demonstrate compliance, leading to failed audits and potential penalties.

- Insufficient employee awareness and training: Employees play a crucial role in maintaining compliance, yet many organizations overlook the importance of security awareness training. Regular training programs ensure that staff members understand regulatory requirements, recognize security threats, and adhere to data protection best practices.

- Failure to implement continuous compliance monitoring: Static compliance models do not account for evolving threats and regulatory updates. Automated compliance tools and real-time monitoring systems help organizations detect and remediate compliance gaps before they escalate into security incidents.

Avoiding these compliance pitfalls requires a strategic approach that incorporates strong governance, continuous risk assessment, and integration of compliance within security operations. Organizations that prioritize proactive compliance management will not only meet regulatory requirements but also strengthen their overall cybersecurity resilience.

## 10.4. Building a Compliance-Driven Security Program

A compliance-driven security program ensures that organizations not only meet regulatory requirements but also strengthen their overall cybersecurity posture. By integrating compliance into security strategies, businesses can mitigate risks, improve resilience, and enhance operational efficiency.

- Security Governance and Accountability: Establishing a governance framework is essential for defining compliance roles, responsibilities, and reporting structures. Organizations should appoint compliance officers, security teams, and risk management personnel to oversee adherence to regulatory mandates and internal policies.

- Continuous Security Assessments: Regular security audits, penetration testing, and vulnerability assessments help organizations identify weaknesses in their compliance programs. Frameworks like ISO 27001 and NIST 800-53 emphasize risk-based assessments to evaluate security effectiveness and ensure continuous improvement.

- Implementation of Security Controls: Organizations must deploy technical controls such as endpoint detection and response (EDR), zero-trust architectures, network segmentation, and secure access policies to meet compliance requirements. Encryption, intrusion prevention systems (IPS), and multi-factor authentication (MFA) further strengthen security defenses.

- Incident Response and Threat Management: Compliance frameworks require businesses to maintain structured incident response plans. Organizations should establish security operations centers (SOCs), automate threat detection with Security Information and Event Management (SIEM) tools, and conduct incident response drills to ensure preparedness for cyber threats.

- Business Alignment and Operational Resilience: Security measures should align with business objectives, ensuring that compliance efforts support operational resilience without disrupting productivity. Adopting security frameworks such as SOC 2 and CIS Controls allows businesses to balance compliance obligations with operational efficiency.

A well-integrated compliance-driven security program ensures that cybersecurity is not just a regulatory requirement but a strategic advantage. Organizations that embed compliance into their broader security strategy can better protect sensitive data, reduce legal exposure, and enhance trust with customers, stakeholders, and regulatory bodies.

# 10.5. Leveraging Compliance as a Service (CaaS) and Automation

Managing compliance requirements can be resource-intensive, requiring organizations to continuously monitor regulatory changes, implement security controls, and prepare for audits. Compliance as a Service (CaaS) provides a structured approach to outsourcing compliance management, allowing organizations to leverage third-party expertise while ensuring adherence to evolving regulatory frameworks. Additionally, Governance, Risk, and Compliance (GRC) automation enables businesses to streamline compliance workflows, enhance security oversight, and improve operational efficiency.

CaaS providers offer specialized services that include policy enforcement, regulatory updates, risk assessments, and audit preparation. By integrating CaaS solutions, organizations can shift compliance management responsibilities to experts who ensure that regulatory obligations are consistently met, reducing the risk of violations and penalties.

- Automated policy enforcement: GRC tools ensure that security configurations and access controls remain aligned with compliance mandates,

reducing the likelihood of misconfigurations that could lead to non-compliance.

- Continuous monitoring: Real-time compliance tracking enables organizations to detect security gaps, unauthorized access attempts, and policy deviations. Automated alerts allow for proactive remediation before compliance violations escalate into security incidents.

- Cloud-based compliance solutions: Organizations operating across multiple jurisdictions benefit from scalable, cloud-based frameworks that centralize compliance management. These solutions streamline policy updates, automate documentation, and provide a unified view of regulatory adherence.

- Automated audit logging and reporting: Compliance frameworks such as ISO 27001, HIPAA, and PCI DSS require detailed audit trails. Automated logging solutions simplify data collection, reducing the time required for audit preparation while ensuring transparency and accountability.

- Risk-based compliance assessments: AI-driven compliance tools analyze regulatory requirements in real time, prioritizing risks based on business impact and compliance gaps. This approach enables organizations to allocate resources more effectively, ensuring that high-priority risks are addressed first.

Leveraging CaaS and automation minimizes manual effort, enhances compliance accuracy, and ensures sustained regulatory adherence. Organizations that implement automated compliance solutions can reduce operational costs, improve security governance, and respond more efficiently to changing regulatory landscapes.

# 10.6. Measuring Compliance Success with Key Performance Indicators

Ensuring regulatory compliance requires continuous evaluation and improvement. Organizations must measure the effectiveness of their compliance programs to assess adherence to security policies, identify weaknesses, and refine security strategies. Key Performance Indicators (KPIs) serve as quantifiable metrics that provide insight into an organization's compliance posture, risk exposure, and overall cybersecurity resilience.

A well-defined compliance measurement strategy involves tracking multiple KPIs across various dimensions of security, governance, and risk management. These metrics enable organizations to validate their security controls, detect policy deviations, and ensure that compliance efforts align with regulatory requirements.

- Audit pass rates: The frequency and success rate of internal and external compliance audits provide a direct measure of regulatory adherence. A high pass rate indicates strong compliance management, while recurring audit failures signal gaps that require remediation.

- Incident response effectiveness: Measuring the organization's ability to detect, contain, and remediate security incidents ensures that compliance frameworks are actively reducing risk. Key indicators include mean time to detect (MTTD), mean time to respond (MTTR), and post-incident reviews.

- Security control adherence: Compliance mandates such as ISO 27001, PCI DSS, and GDPR require strict security controls, including encryption, access control, and data protection measures. Monitoring adherence to these controls ensures compliance objectives are met and risks are mitigated.

- Employee security awareness levels: Human error is a leading cause of security breaches. Regular security awareness training, phishing simulation results, and policy adherence rates provide insight into the effectiveness of cybersecurity training programs.

- Data protection and privacy metrics: GDPR and CCPA require organizations to track the number of access requests, data deletion requests, and breach notifications. Analyzing these metrics helps ensure compliance with privacy laws and regulatory obligations.

- Vendor and third-party compliance: Organizations must ensure that third-party vendors and service providers comply with security standards. Conducting vendor risk assessments and tracking third-party audit compliance rates can help reduce supply chain vulnerabilities.

- Policy and procedure effectiveness: Measuring the adoption and enforcement of security policies ensures that compliance initiatives are effectively integrated into daily business operations. Metrics such as policy violation rates and remediation timelines highlight areas requiring improvement.

Regularly evaluating these KPIs allows organizations to take a proactive approach to compliance, ensuring that security measures remain effective and aligned with evolving regulatory requirements. By leveraging these performance indicators, organizations can improve security governance, reduce regulatory risk, and enhance their overall cybersecurity resilience.

## 10.7. Q&A Section

Q: What is the importance of compliance standards when security cannot be achieved through compliance alone?

A: Basic security controls from compliance measures serve as minimum requirements despite continuous changes in cyber threats. Organizations need to combine regulatory requirements with aggressive threat intelligence functions, continuous monitoring systems, and flexible defence protocols.

Q: Businesses, at what rate must they perform compliance audits?

A: An annual audit procedure must be implemented, and organizations need to perform extra assessments when they implement substantial system alterations, experience regulatory changes, or experience a security incident.

Q: What consequences do failure to comply with cybersecurity regulations result in?

A: Per regulation, the penalties can differ from one another. Organizations that violate GDPR may face fines equivalent to four per cent of their worldwide revenue, whereas organizations violating HIPAA can experience penalties that exceed millions of dollars. Legally acceptable penalties, alongside significant harm to reputation and the complete breakdown of customer trust, can affect organizations.

Q: What are the best approaches that small businesses can use to implement compliance requirements with their limited budgets?

A: Smaller business entities need to prioritize their investments in essential security components, which include protected entry systems, encryption features, and worker education about cybersecurity threats. Cost reduction occurs through cloud-based security services and outsourcing compliance testing operations.

Q: Are compliance requirements the same across industries?

A: The compliance standards of different business sectors remain independent. Organizations dealing with healthcare must follow HIPAA regulations, while financial institutions need to comply with SOX and PCI DSS requirements, and federal contractors need to follow NIST standards.

# Part IV.

# Future Consideration

# 11. Artificial Intelligence, Cloud Security, and the Future of Compliance

Security operations benefit from AI's ability to detect threats while optimizing risk management and establishing automated processes for compliance needs. Current enterprises require Cloud Security (CS) to achieve optimal security outcomes through the Cloud Security Alliance (CSA), the Federal Risk and Authorization Management Program (FedRAMP), and the Cloud Computing Compliance Controls Catalog (C5), which set security guidelines for cloud infrastructure protection. Cloud service customers and CSPs must have specific security duties defined through the Shared Responsibility Model (SRM) for cloud computing operations to ensure regulatory compliance. Organizations must handle ethical matters and regulatory obstacles while dealing with shifting cyber dangers and implementing AI-powered compliance workflows. This section reveals upcoming AI security trends, cloud compliance practices, automated governance, and the best standards for security resilience in quickly transforming digital environments.

## 11.1. Artificial Intelligence-Driven Security Solutions and Compliance

Artificial Intelligence (AI) transforms cybersecurity and compliance through automated threat detection, risk assessment automation, and improved governance framework optimization. Security technologies powered by AI examine enormous security data collections to reveal normal patterns, detect abnormal events, and forecast impending security risks ahead of time. The detection-based security approach builds cyberspace resilience and decreases security staff workload to improve regulatory adherence.

Organizations that use conventional security systems identify threats by relying on established rules. With AI, security incidents and new attack methods become learnable components for developing improved risk models in an adaptive security environment. Through Machine Learning (ML) algorithm implementation, intrusion detection systems gain better accuracy by identifying differences between normal network behaviours. The AI processing capability of Natural Language Processing enables computers to read security logs, compliance reports, and policy documents to identify regulatory gaps and verify security standard compliance.

Implementing Artificial Intelligence leads to significant improvements in operations related to compliance management. Organizations need constant monitoring and reporting under the regulatory standards represented by GDPR, HIPAA, and PCI-DSS. AI-driven tools that examine policy changes originate from real-time detection, audit report generation, and policy compliance analysis. The system reduces the possibility of regulatory sanctions and improves governance transparency.

Cloud security functions significantly better because of AI automation systems. Cloud environments produce extreme quantities of access logs, configuration data, and network activity. Wizard algorithms scan the collected information to identify security misconfigurations, unauthorized access, and policy violation incidents. The cloud computing security model, the Shared Responsibility Model (SRM), requires companies to adhere to security best practices for compliance. With AI solutions, organizations can monitor multi-cloud compliance points, which enhances security management by reducing the frequency of data breaches.

Artificial intelligence enhances the strength of identity and access management operations. Behavioural analytic systems identify irregularities in routine employee actions, which disclose internal risks regarding staff misconduct and unauthorized password use. Combining Multi-Factor Authentication (MFA) with artificial intelligence risk assessment improves user identity verification security. Role-based access controls use AI to change user permissions immediately when security risks appear during real-time operations.

AI technology creates security challenges alongside compliance issues for cybersecurity systems. Security operations must maintain explainable AI-driven decisions to allow for proper accountability within security operations. The system will likely produce mistaken results when training data contains biases, leading to unnecessary negative evaluations. Organizations should develop complicated governance mechanisms to track AI system conduct, test algorithm precision, and set guidelines for automated decision systems.

Information technology adoption in cybersecurity increases steadily because organizations use it to boost security capabilities while automating threat recognition and meeting regulatory standards. The integration of responsible AI governance solutions will enable businesses to guarantee transparency, accurate operations, and fair security practices. Organizations must maintain constant surveillance as AI capabilities progress to maintain effective innovation with necessary security and compliance measures.

## 11.2. Automating Compliance Workflows with Artificial Intelligence and Machine Learning

Machine Learning (ML) and Artificial Intelligence (AI) evolve compliance management through automated processes which decrease human effort while raising security standards through better accuracy and steady regulatory compliance. The current compliance system uses manual tracking with extensive documentation alongside auditing, creating resource challenges and human error potential. These tasks become streamlined because AI-automatic systems analyze regulatory requirements, establish security control diagrams and offer instant monitoring solutions.

Organizations use automated compliance tools to fulfil requirements set by regulatory standards, including GDPR, HIPAA, and PCI-DSS. These tools carry out automatic policy scanning and gap detection to provide organizations with proper recommendation solutions that enable regulatory maintenance according to current standards.

Organizations achieve improved audit management because of AI automation functions. Standard audits demand employees to conduct manual assessments of system logs together with policy documents and configuration details. Automation through AI technology creates audit reports, manages compliance measurements, and reports security breaches to users. Organizations utilizing Security Information and Event Management (SIEM) systems that link with AI technology process real-time information to warn about compliance breaches together with unapproved system modifications. Preparing audits through this method reduces time and improves accuracy in reports.

AI helps policy enforcement by maintaining uniform security controls throughout every organization's network system. AI-driven systems manage access permission monitoring and unauthorized data access detection functions alongside encryption policy execution. The system sends automated notifications to agreed-upon compliance teams to show when control deviations occur so teams can act immediately to solve them. Such measures enable organizations to satisfy industry standards and minimize human errors.

Integrating AI produces better compliance cost efficiency by eliminating manual process requirements. Implementing automated workflows helps organizations evaluate risks, generate required regulatory documentation, and support incident response development. Organizations achieve cost efficiency through the implementation of AI-driven compliance management platforms that link with their current security frameworks.

AI automation provides real-time compliance monitoring because of its essential advantages. Organizations experience regulatory violations between standard compliance audits because their checks occur at set intervals. System configuration monitoring, user activity surveillance, and data security policy enforcement occur in real-time through AI, maintaining continuous compliance detection. Through anomaly detection technologies, systems discover unordinary activities to notify potential violations that could grow into compliance problems.

Machine Learning algorithms boost security compliance efficiency through their ability to analyze historical events, which enhances security system operations. Predictive analytics enables companies to detect upcoming compliance risks through which they can establish preventive measures. Online tools that operate under artificial intelligence base their analysis on recent updates in regulatory laws to keep businesses updated on new requirements.

Organizations need to handle AI-driven compliance automation processes with care because of their numerous advantages. System organizations must execute verifications on AI-made compliance documents, fix possible biases within machine learning systems, and maintain automation detail in decision-making methods. Governance frameworks need structured oversight systems to accomplish accountable regulatory compliance.

AI technology and ML systems transform compliance workflows through automated system auditing, cost-cutting, and enhanced policy control functions. Organizations using AI-driven automation systems will achieve higher accuracy and organizational resilience while enhancing their compliance management efficiency.

## 11.3. Ethical Considerations and Risks of Artificial Intelligence in Governance, Risk, and Compliance

Organizations need to tackle ethical problems caused by growing Artificial Intelligence in Governance, Risk, and Compliance deployments because they face security model bias, decision-making transparency, and compliance enforcement accountability issues. Using Artificial Intelligence for increased efficiency requires organizations to face and properly control the serious risks it creates.

The major issue deriving from automated decision-making involves the occurrence of biased outcomes. The training data used by Machine Learning models can potentially cause unfair security assessments when biased information exists within the data. Such improper patterns within security systems result in incorrect threat alerts, causing users to be placed into inappropriate classifications. Regular Artificial Intelligence model auditing should accompany diverse training data samplings and fairness assessment methods to reduce discriminatory outcomes.

One major challenge arises when security enforcement systems conduct operations without adequate disclosure. Complex algorithms used by Artificial Intelligence-driven systems produce operations that are not easily understood by human observers. Security teams need a full understanding of why an Artificial Intelligence system makes a compliance decision or detects a security incident. Systems should implement Explainable Artificial Intelligence, which provides detailed explanations when risk categories are determined while policy execution actions become clear to users.

Security operations that depend on Artificial Intelligence must have total accountability as its core principle. The reports and access controls, alongside policy violation detection of automated compliance tools, might contain errors. Identifying accountability becomes challenging when Artificial Intelligence generates wrong security evaluations or ignores possible threats. Organizations should prioritize developing oversight systems that explain artificial intelligence decision review protocols and assign complete responsibility for Artificial Intelligence-driven choices.

Large amounts of sensitive security data become a privacy problem when Artificial Intelligence systems analyze and process this data. Artificial Intelligence solutions process security data from logs, network traffic, and access records, exposing confidential organizational business information to risk. Since artificial intelligence systems get compromised, they become vulnerable to cyberattacks and expose data to leaks. Organizations should protect their data through effective measures and strict data collection boundaries, and they should force artificial intelligence security models to respect privacy regulations.

Organizations must evaluate the potential problems from too heavily depending on automation systems. Automated systems can detect established threat patterns, while new cybersecurity threats typically need human decision-making to analyze properly. Implementing complete automation in security creates potential weak points where Artificial Intelligence cannot detect fresh attack approaches. Businesses must combine Artificial Intelligence with human security professionals who will work together rather than substitute people for machines.

Regulatory compliance frameworks adapt to create governance guidelines for Artificial Intelligence security systems. New laws, together with policies, stress the importance of maintaining fair practices in addition to accountable systems that prioritize transparent automated computations. Organizations that employ Artificial Intelligence for compliance and security operations need to follow established regulatory compliance expectations as a requirement for both trust with stakeholders and legal compliance.

Businesses should develop appropriate Artificial Intelligence governance policies to reduce such risks. The necessary steps for risk management involve regular model testing alongside better decision transparency and human supervision for systems that depend on Artificial Intelligence security operations. Organizations must deploy Artificial Intelligence tools ethically while establishing proper safeguards and fair application methods.

Organizations can achieve many benefits from Artificial Intelligence in Governance, Risk, and Compliance as they diligently manage their ethical risks. Artificial intelligence efficiently serves organizations for ethical cybersecurity practices through bias reduction and transparent operations backed by regulatory compliance and ongoing accountability.

# 11.4. Securing Cloud Environments: Amazon Web Services, Microsoft Azure, Google Cloud Platform

Cloud environment protection is vital because enterprises continue shifting their operations to cloud-based systems. Amazon Web Services, Microsoft Azure, and Google Cloud Platform include security tools for their platforms, although security and regulatory compliance responsibilities lie between platform owners and their customers. Strong security measures have become mandatory for organizations to safeguard sensitive data structures, stop unauthorized access, and follow regulatory frameworks.

According to the shared responsibility model definition, cloud computing security responsibilities lie between providers and customers. Cloud service providers defend the physical elements of data centres, including networks and storage equipment. Customers are responsible for application security, data protection, identity protection, and configuration safety. A secure cloud requires a complete understanding of the roles providers and customers must fulfil.

Identity and access management stand out as the crucial element among all security measures in cloud computing. Cloud providers furnish security tools that help organizations implement role-based access control and enforce limited access privileges through the Multi-Factor Authentication framework. Organizations should perform job-based access control followed by identity verification before providing authorization permissions to limit unauthorized entry.

Data protection functions as a main component of cloud security systems. Every organization needs to apply data encryption methods to protect information when it sits inactive and when it moves between systems. The encryption services that cloud platforms deliver help businesses safeguard their sensitive information to defend against unauthorized access attempts. Organizations use data classification policies to decide which data types need maximum security measures.

Security groups, firewalls, and virtual private networks need proper configuration to maintain network security in cloud environments. Cloud platforms enable businesses to protect their network traffic through three major security tools: distributed denial-of-service protection and intrusion detection systems with web application firewalls. Organizations need to perform periodic checks of their network security parameters to avoid security holes and maintain their current status.

Improper configuration settings compromise the security of cloud environments, which frequently occurs as an organizational risk. Security misconfiguration issues make cloud applications and essential data vulnerable to public exposure. Security automated assessment platforms help organizations find misconfigurations while automatically enforcing security best practices. To preserve cloud environment security, businesses must conduct periodic security audits and compliance checks.

Security incidents and their response processes are essential elements supporting cloud security operations. Cloud service providers give their customers access to monitoring software tools that enable them to track down and handle security threats. Businesses benefit from real-time threat detection capabilities alongside automated response mechanisms, which decrease security incident damage.

Organizations must follow cloud security frameworks because they serve as necessary standards to fulfil industry and regulatory obligations. The Cloud Security Alliance guidelines, the Federal Risk and Authorization Management Program, and the Cloud Computing Compliance Controls Catalog deliver established security practices for cloud environments. Organizations must adopt security frameworks to support their procedures and achieve regulatory requirements.

The growing adoption of cloud computing requires businesses to initiate preventive measures to secure their systems. Organizations can minimize security risks while improving cloud protection through rigorous identity access measures, encryption protocols, network protection systems, and continuous assessment procedures. Cloud infrastructure operations gain security and compliance through a clear understanding of the shared responsibility model and implementation of a security framework.

## 11.5. The Shared Responsibility Model and Cloud Compliance

According to the shared responsibility model, cloud computing security obligations are split into two responsibilities between customers and cloud service providers. Cloud service providers defend the core infrastructure comprising data centres, hardware components, and network systems. All data protection and application security responsibilities lie with the customer, identity access management and configuration control. IT security professionals need to correctly execute the shared responsibility model to preserve cloud-based security alongside regulatory compliance.

Companies that employ cloud services must verify that their security protocols fulfil their compliance quotas. Security standards expressed through the General Data Protection Regulation, Health Insurance Portability and Accountability Act and Payment Card Industry Data Security Standard enforce strict protections for sensitive data. Businesses must modify cloud system configurations to fulfil security regulations and establish clear security assignment protocols.

Cloud customers must manage identity and access responsibilities as their primary cloud security duties. Organizations must set up role-based access control with least privilege access permissions and Multi-Factor Authentication to stop unauthorized system access. Users need to precisely configure identity management tools from cloud service providers to minimize security risks during implementation.

Encryption directly supports the protection of cloud-stored data and cloud-processed information. Cloud platforms enable data protection through encryption services that defend information while it rests on the system and while it moves between networks. Organizations need to apply robust encryption rules and key administration solutions to comply with data protection standards.

A cloud environment requires continuous monitoring for security threat detection and response operations. Cloud providers deliver monitoring tools that enable businesses to document user actions and follow abnormal patterns while responding to incidents during real-time activities. Access to security logs requires customers to activate them while conducting periodic checks to identify security risks.

Organizations benefit from compliance automation tools to run continuous monitoring that keeps their cloud infrastructure safe and in regulatory compliance. Cloud platforms offer security framework automation that monitors configuration analysis while finding security violations before generating regulatory audit reports. Organizations' security workflows must adopt these tools for continuous regulatory compliance.

The misconfiguration of security features stands out as the main cloud environment risk. Computing cloud service users need to perform routine security audits to find instances of uncontrolled storage permissions, inactive access controls, and substandard authentication protocols. Security scanning automation enables organizations to locate and repair critical system weaknesses.

The cloud compliance frameworks deliver standardized procedures for securing workloads in the cloud environment. The Cloud Security Alliance, together with the Federal Risk and Authorization Management Program and Cloud Computing Compliance Controls Catalog, offers organizations standardized security principles for implementation. Companies must synchronize their security guidelines with these control guidelines to achieve compliance and shield themselves from regulatory consequences.

Organizations achieve their cloud security obligations by properly implementing the shared responsibility model. Secure identity access, data encryption, continuous monitoring, and compliance framework alignment ensure businesses can operate in a safe and standardized cloud system.

# 12. Zero Trust, Cybersecurity Evolution, and Future Trends

The next section analyzes Zero Trust security as an advanced cybersecurity structure and explores how it meets regulatory standards. Under the Zero Trust security model, different elements are foundational because they require mandatory identity authentication and limited user permissions while systems check continuously to block unauthorized users. The section studies current cybersecurity changes by examining three technological advancements: Quantum Computing, Internet of Things devices, and five-generation mobile networks (5G). Understanding future cybersecurity developments together with upcoming regulations delivers essential insights about risk management and compliance procedures in evolution. Organizations can better face upcoming cybersecurity threats by understanding current technological developments.

# 12.1. How Zero Trust Security Models Fit into Compliance Strategies

All assets within the Zero Trust Architecture require ongoing verification to obtain access permissions since the framework defaults to the nonautomatic trust of users or devices. The security standards enact full identity verification while implementing restricted permissions and dividing network domains. Through Zero Trust deployment, organizations achieve complete regulatory compliance while operating with peak cybersecurity standards.

The traditional security frameworks automatically grant trust status to users and devices located inside internal networks. The present security model shows vulnerabilities when it comes to defending against attacks started by staff members within the organization or incidents involving credential theft and informal network port movement protocols. Every device request under Zero Trust Architecture demands authentication and authorization before gaining access to any system, regardless of its network position.

Organizations must create access restrictions under GDPR HIP, AA, and PCI DSS requirements to protect data while conducting regular security monitoring tasks. Zero Trust applies security principles that match generalized compliance framework needs because authorized users and devices receive access to protected electronic assets. When deployed, the framework protects against unauthorized entry, thus enabling organizations to accomplish better regulatory goals.

The core principle of Zero Trust involves building security through least privilege access enforcement. Operating entities must establish role-based access control systems and systematic restrictions on user permission levels that match the requirements of their duties. They also need to monitor access privileges regularly. Through authorization restrictions, businesses reduce security risks and fulfil essential compliance obligations related to access control.

Micro-segmentation establishes multiple zone boundaries throughout networks, protecting them from security threats that attempt to spread between areas. When an attacker breaches a device, the security approach of micro-segmentation still blocks access to different important systems. All security standards requiring protected data environments are compatible with this security framework.

Real-time threat detection and continuous monitoring are fundamental to the Zero Trust security framework. Through Security Information, Event Management systems, and behavioural analytics, organizations can identify unwanted behaviours while preventing unauthorized access attempts to take fast security actions. Security assessments required by compliance regulations become possible due to Zero Trust, which continuously verifies network activity patterns.

Zero Trust Architecture increases compliance automation through its combined platform, which integrates security controls for managing identities, encryption systems, and network defences. Basic compliance audits become less complex for Zero Trust-implementing organizations because they maintain forensic-quality access records alongside automated policies and security response systems.

Organizations must implement Zero Trust because it has become essential to satisfy regulatory compliance needs in an era of changing cyber threats. Adopting this model strengthens security governance, improves access control systems, and leads to compliance with framework requirements based on risk-based security models. Implementing Zero Trust leads organizations to achieve better cybersecurity strength and adherence to regulations.

## 12.2. Implementing Zero Trust for Identity, Access, and Network Security

Using Zero Trust principles helps improve identity, access, and network security. It reduces the risk of unauthorized access by ensuring that every user is constantly checked and follows strict rules. Identity and access management are key in Zero Trust. Companies need to verify who a user is every time they access something. Multi-factor authentication adds extra steps for security. Role-based access control ensures users only access what they need. Also, adaptive authentication checks the safety of devices and locations to boost security. For access control, Zero Trust gives the least privilege. Organizations should set clear rules for access, regularly check permissions, and remove unnecessary ones. Just-in-time access allows temporary access to resources only when necessary.

These steps help keep unwanted users out and comply with data protection rules. Network security in Zero Trust breaks networks into smaller parts. If an attacker tries to enter, they cannot move easily between sections. Each section has its own security rules to control how systems communicate. Secure network access ensures that users and devices are verified before reaching internal resources. Keeping an eye on everything for threats is vital in Zero Trust. Security tools collect logs to spot unusual activities. Behavioural analytics can alert teams to strange user actions. Automated responses help organizations act fast against potential threats. Cloud security also benefits from Zero Trust. Strict access rules and ongoing checks protect cloud workloads. Cloud platforms use identity-based policies to limit access to sensitive data. By following Zero Trust, companies can keep their cloud spaces safe from unauthorized access.

It is important to regularly check and improve Zero Trust strategies to stay ahead of new threats. Businesses should assess their security often, update access rules, and use automation to help with Zero Trust goals. As regulations require strong access controls and constant monitoring, Zero Trust meets those demands and helps enhance security. Companies using Zero Trust for identity, access, and network security can lower security risks and better comply with industry rules. This approach promotes safety at every level of an organization's digital setup.

# 12.3. Regulatory Implications of Zero Trust Network Access

Zero Trust Network Access is becoming popular as a security model. It helps control who can access information and lowers cybersecurity risks. As rules change, many regulations now see how useful Zero Trust Network Access is. It boosts data safety, stops unauthorized access, and keeps an eye on security all the time. Companies must link their Zero Trust strategies with these rules to stay compliant and enhance security. Laws like the General Data Protection Regulation, Health Insurance Portability and Accountability Act, and Payment Card Industry Data Security Standard have strict rules about who can access data, how to protect it, and how to track user activity. Zero Trust Network Access meets these needs by insisting on identity checks, limiting access to sensitive areas, and showing real-time network activity.

Checking identities is key to following the law. Zero Trust Network Access helps with this by needing proof of identity each time someone tries to get in. Tools like Multi-Factor Authentication and risk-based access policies help organizations meet the strict identity rules. By confirming users and devices before letting them in, companies lower the chances of data breaches. Continuous monitoring and security logs are also a must for compliance. Zero Trust Network Access gives detailed records of access attempts, policy actions, and security events. These logs help with audits, making it easier for companies to show they care about following the rules regarding access control. Data protection laws require strong measures for dealing with sensitive information.

Zero Trust Network Access limits risk exposure by controlling who can access applications and data. It considers things like user roles and device safety. Micro-segmentation boosts security even more by blocking access between internal systems, which stops threats from moving around. Compliance automation tools that work with Zero Trust Network Access make it easier for companies to follow the rules. They check security setups, enforce access policies, and produce compliance reports automatically. This reduces the hassle of doing compliance manually and helps ensure that security policies meet changing standards. To adopt Zero Trust Network Access, businesses need to refresh their security policies and ensure they fit the rules. They should regularly check their compliance, document access policies, and set up automated security monitoring. Training security teams on Zero Trust ideas and rules help ensure the proper use of the policies. As rules focus more on strong access controls and adaptive security, Zero Trust Network Access offers a clear way to stay compliant. Businesses using Zero Trust in their security setups improve compliance, decrease cybersecurity risks, and strengthen access management.

## 12.4. Trends Shaping Cybersecurity Compliance: Quantum Computing, Internet of Things, and 5G Security

Technology keeps changing the world of cybersecurity. New tools like Quantum Computing, the Internet of Things (IoT), and 5G bring fresh security risks and challenges. Businesses must change their security plans to keep up with these fast-moving threats and meet regulations. Quantum Computing is a big deal. It could crack encryption methods that keep our data safe. This creates serious risks for data security. Because of this, regulators are pushing for Quantum-Resistant Cryptography. This means businesses need to start using new encryption methods to stay safe in the future.

IoT devices are everywhere now, which means there is a higher chance of cyberattacks. These devices often do not have strong security, making them easy targets. Compliance rules are getting stricter. Businesses must use strong passwords and encrypted communication and keep an eye on these devices to protect themselves. Regulations like the General Data Protection Regulation focus on data and device security as the use of IoT grows. 5G networks offer super-fast data speeds but come with new risks. How these networks are built can create weak points that hackers might exploit.

Regulators are stepping in with guidelines to protect

5G networks, focusing on supply chain security and data privacy. Companies must update their security policies to keep up with these new standards. Businesses are turning to automation and AI-driven security systems to manage the risks of new tech. These tools help with real-time threat detection and ensure compliance with new security rules. Automated systems make it easier for organizations to adapt to changing regulations and keep monitoring for threats. As cybersecurity laws change, businesses must stay proactive. Preparing for new encryption standards, securing IoT devices, and protecting 5G networks are key steps to staying compliant in the future.

## 12.5. Predictions for the Next Decade in Governance, Risk, and Compliance

Governance, Risk, and Compliance will see big changes in the next decade. This is mainly because of tougher rules, better AI in security, and new ways to manage risks. As cyber threats get more complicated, companies must adapt their compliance to stay safe. Expect more rules to come down the pipeline. Governments will tighten data protection laws. New rules will focus on AI management, data ownership, and supply chain safety. Companies must prepare using tools that automate compliance and keep up with real-time legal changes. AI will be important for managing Governance, Risk, and Compliance. Predictive analytics and automated monitoring can help with risk assessments and reduce manual audits. With security automation, compliance workflows will get easier. They can continuously check security setups, find weaknesses, and create instant compliance reports. Zero Trust security will likely become a standard. As cyberattacks improve, businesses must enforce strict access controls, ongoing user verification, and segmented networks. Compliance rules will push for zero-trust practices to ensure secure identity management and limited access. Quantum computing will bring new problems to data security. Outdated encryption methods may no longer work, so businesses must shift to stronger, quantum-resistant encryption. Compliance rules will soon require these new techniques to keep sensitive data safe. More cloud services and remote work will create fresh security challenges. Compliance standards will adapt to cover issues like multi-cloud risks, data transfers between countries, and monitoring in cloud environments. Companies should create flexible compliance strategies that can work with cloud setups. AI and machine learning will also help with fraud detection, regulatory reports, and risk assessments, making Governance, Risk, and Compliance more efficient. Automated systems will help companies spot policy breaches, stick to rules, and manage compliance risks as they happen. As things change, businesses need to think ahead about security and compliance. Those who use AI in security, adopt Zero Trust, and use quantum-safe encryption will boost their security and keep up with future regulations.

# 12.6. Final Thoughts and Call to Action for Security Professionals

As cyber threats become more sophisticated, security professionals must take a proactive approach to cybersecurity and compliance. Governance, Risk, and Compliance frameworks must evolve to address emerging risks, regulatory changes, and advancements in artificial intelligence-driven security operations. Organizations that integrate security automation, continuous monitoring, and adaptive risk management will enhance their resilience against cyber threats.

Security professionals should prioritize the implementation of Zero Trust principles. Strict identity verification, least privilege access, and continuous authentication should be enforced across all systems. Microsegmentation and real-time threat detection must be integrated to minimize attack surfaces and prevent lateral movement of cyber threats.

Artificial intelligence-driven security solutions should be leveraged to automate compliance monitoring, detect anomalies, and strengthen security policies. Machine learning algorithms can improve threat intelligence, automate security assessments, and enhance regulatory compliance reporting. Security professionals must ensure that artificial intelligence models are transparent, bias-free, and aligned with ethical governance frameworks.

Cloud security compliance should remain a top priority. Organizations must enforce strong identity management, implement encryption for data protection, and continuously monitor cloud security configurations. The shared responsibility model should be clearly defined to ensure security responsibilities are properly assigned between cloud providers and customers.

Security awareness training and a strong cybersecurity culture must be fostered within organizations. Employees should be educated on cybersecurity best practices, phishing prevention, and compliance requirements. Human error remains a significant cybersecurity risk, and ongoing training can reduce vulnerabilities related to social engineering attacks.

Security professionals must stay informed about evolving regulatory requirements, emerging threats, and industry best practices. Continuous learning, participation in cybersecurity communities, and collaboration with regulatory bodies will help organizations maintain compliance and adapt to new security challenges.

Governance, Risk, and Compliance is a continuous process that requires security professionals to remain vigilant, proactive, and adaptable. By integrating automation, Zero Trust security, and regulatory compliance strategies, organizations can build a resilient cybersecurity framework that protects sensitive data, mitigates risks, and ensures long-term security success.

# Glossary of Cybersecurity and Compliance Terms

This glossary provides definitions for key terms related to cybersecurity, risk management, and compliance. Understanding these terms is essential for professionals navigating security regulations, governance frameworks, and evolving cyber threats.

- **Artificial Intelligence (AI)** – The use of machine learning and algorithms to automate cybersecurity processes, threat detection, and compliance monitoring.

- **Access Control** – Security measures that regulate who or what can access data, applications, and systems based on identity verification.

- **Authentication** – The process of verifying a user's identity before granting access to a system or resource.

- **Cloud Computing** – The delivery of computing services, such as storage and processing power, over the internet instead of on-premises infrastructure.

- **Compliance Framework** – A structured set of guidelines, policies, and controls designed to help organizations meet security and regulatory requirements.

- **Cyber Threat** – Any malicious act that seeks to damage, steal, or disrupt digital assets and infrastructure.

- **Data Encryption** – A method of securing sensitive data by converting it into an unreadable format that can only be decrypted with a valid key.

- **Endpoint Security** – Measures taken to secure individual devices such as computers, mobile phones, and Internet of Things devices from cyber threats.

- **Firewall** – A network security system that monitors and controls incoming and outgoing network traffic based on security rules.

- **Governance, Risk, and Compliance (GRC)** – An integrated approach to managing an organization's security policies, risk management strategies, and regulatory compliance.

- **Health Insurance Portability and Accountability Act (HIPAA)** – A United States regulation that protects sensitive healthcare data and ensures privacy for patients.

- **Identity and Access Management (IAM)** – Security practices that ensure the right individuals access the right resources at the right time.

- **Intrusion Detection System (IDS)** – A security solution that monitors network traffic for suspicious activity or known cyber threats.

- **Least Privilege Access** – A security principle that restricts users' access to only the resources they need to perform their tasks.

- **Multi-Factor Authentication (MFA)** – A security measure that requires multiple forms of verification to authenticate a user.

- **National Institute of Standards and Technology Cybersecurity Framework (NIST CSF)** – A cybersecurity framework that provides best practices for managing cyber risks.

- **Payment Card Industry Data Security Standard (PCI-DSS)** – A global standard that ensures the secure handling of payment card transactions.

- **Phishing** – A cyberattack method where attackers impersonate trusted entities to trick users into revealing sensitive information.

- **Quantum Computing** – An emerging technology that has the potential to break traditional encryption methods, requiring the adoption of quantum-resistant cryptographic techniques.

- **Risk Assessment** – The process of identifying, analyzing, and mitigating cybersecurity risks in an organization.

- **Security Information and Event Management (SIEM)** – A system that collects and analyzes security data to detect, investigate, and respond to cyber threats.

- **Shared Responsibility Model** – A security framework that defines security obligations between cloud service providers and customers.

- **Threat Intelligence** – The collection and analysis of information to understand cyber threats and prevent potential attacks.

- **Zero Trust Architecture (ZTA)** – A security model that eliminates implicit trust and requires continuous verification of all users and devices attempting to access resources.

This glossary serves as a reference for key cybersecurity and compliance terms used throughout this book. Understanding these concepts is essential for professionals responsible for securing enterprise environments and ensuring compliance with evolving regulatory standards.

# Templates for Policies, Risk Assessment Checklists, and Compliance Roadmaps

This chapter provides structured templates that organizations can use to develop cybersecurity policies, conduct risk assessments, and implement compliance roadmaps. These templates serve as practical tools for security professionals, risk managers, and compliance officers to ensure consistency, efficiency, and alignment with regulatory standards.

## 1. Cybersecurity Policy Template

Organizations need well-defined security policies to establish guidelines for data protection, access control, and incident response. The following template provides a structured approach to drafting a cybersecurity policy.

# Policy Title: [Enter Policy Name]

## Purpose:

The purpose of this policy is to establish clear guidelines for securing organizational assets, protecting sensitive data, and ensuring compliance with relevant security standards and regulations. This policy defines the security requirements necessary to safeguard information systems against unauthorized access, cyber threats, and data breaches. It provides a structured approach for managing security risks while supporting business continuity and regulatory adherence.

## Scope:

This policy applies to all employees, contractors, third-party vendors, and any individuals who have access to the organization's information systems, networks, and digital resources. It covers all computing devices, cloud environments, databases, and communication systems used within the organization. The policy also extends to on-premises and remote work environments, ensuring consistent security practices across all operational areas.

## Roles and Responsibilities:

- **Security Team:** Responsible for implementing, enforcing, and reviewing security policies.

- **Employees:** Expected to adhere to security guidelines, report suspicious activities, and follow best practices.

- **IT Department:** Ensures security controls are properly configured, updated, and monitored.

- **Third-Party Vendors:** Must comply with organizational security policies and data protection standards.

## Security Controls:

- Implementation of Multi-Factor Authentication for system access.

- Encryption of sensitive data at rest and in transit.

- Regular software updates and patch management.

- Firewall and intrusion detection system deployment.

- Secure password management policies and periodic password rotation.

## Incident Response Plan:

- Identification and classification of security incidents.

- Immediate containment and mitigation strategies.

- Investigation and root cause analysis.

- Notification procedures for regulatory authorities and stakeholders.

- Documentation and post-incident review for future prevention.

## Compliance and Enforcement:

Non-compliance with this policy may result in disciplinary action, including revocation of system access, legal action, or termination of contracts. Regular audits will be conducted to ensure adherence to policy requirements.

## Review and Updates:

This policy shall be reviewed annually or when significant changes occur in the security landscape or regulatory requirements.

# 2. Risk Assessment Checklist

A structured risk assessment checklist helps organizations identify, evaluate, and mitigate cybersecurity risks. The following checklist provides a systematic approach to risk assessment.

# Risk Assessment Categories:

- Identify and classify critical assets, including sensitive data and infrastructure components.

- Assess potential cybersecurity threats, including insider risks, malware, and data breaches.

- Evaluate existing security controls and their effectiveness in mitigating identified risks.

- Determine vulnerabilities in software, network configurations, and third-party integrations.

- Analyze potential business impact in case of security incidents.

- Prioritize risks based on their likelihood and severity.

- Develop mitigation strategies, such as security control enhancements and staff training.

- Establish monitoring mechanisms for continuous risk assessment.

- Ensure alignment with regulatory requirements such as General Data Protection Regulation, Payment Card Industry Data Security Standard, and Health Insurance Portability and Accountability Act.

# 3. Compliance Roadmap Template

A compliance roadmap helps organizations track their progress in meeting regulatory requirements. The following template provides a structured approach to implementing compliance initiatives.

## Regulatory Frameworks:

Organizations should identify and align with relevant compliance standards, including:

- General Data Protection Regulation

- Payment Card Industry Data Security Standard

- Health Insurance Portability and Accountability Act

- National Institute of Standards and Technology Cybersecurity Framework

- Federal Risk and Authorization Management Program

- Cloud Computing Compliance Controls Catalog

- Cloud Security Alliance Guidelines

## Compliance Objectives:

Clearly define compliance objectives and regulatory expectations, including:

- Protecting personal and sensitive data.

- Ensuring secure access controls.

- Implementing effective incident response mechanisms.

- Conducting regular security risk assessments.

- Maintaining regulatory audit readiness.


## Implementation Plan:

- Perform a compliance gap analysis to assess current security posture.

- Develop and enforce security policies aligned with compliance standards.

- Implement technical controls, such as encryption, endpoint security, and access management.

- Establish security awareness training programs for employees.

- Deploy continuous monitoring and security logging mechanisms.

- Define an incident response plan to address compliance violations and cyber incidents.

## Monitoring and Continuous Improvement:

To ensure ongoing compliance, organizations should:

- Conduct periodic audits and security reviews.

- Update security policies and compliance documentation based on regulatory changes.

- Implement security automation to streamline compliance processes.

- Maintain detailed logs of compliance activities for audit purposes.

- Establish a compliance governance team responsible for overseeing regulatory adherence.

These templates provide a structured approach for organizations to develop and implement cybersecurity policies, conduct risk assessments, and establish compliance roadmaps. By following these frameworks, security professionals can enhance cybersecurity resilience, reduce regulatory risks, and ensure effective security governance.

# Additional Resources and Recommended Readings

Cybersecurity, risk management, and compliance are continuously evolving fields. Staying informed about the latest developments, frameworks, and best practices is essential for security professionals. This chapter provides a curated list of additional resources, including industry standards, regulatory guidelines, research papers, and books that offer deeper insights into cybersecurity governance, risk management, and compliance.

## 1. Cybersecurity Frameworks and Guidelines

- **National Institute of Standards and Technology Cybersecurity Framework (NIST CSF)** – A widely adopted framework for managing cybersecurity risks and improving security posture.

- **General Data Protection Regulation (GDPR)** – European data protection regulations that outline privacy and security requirements for handling personal data.

- **Payment Card Industry Data Security Standard (PCI-DSS)** – A compliance standard for securing payment card transactions.

- **Health Insurance Portability and Accountability Act (HIPAA)** – Regulations focused on protecting healthcare data and ensuring privacy.

- **Federal Risk and Authorization Management Program (FedRAMP)** – A security assessment framework for cloud service providers handling government data.

- **Cloud Security Alliance (CSA) Guidelines** – Best practices for securing cloud computing environments.

- **Zero Trust Architecture (ZTA)** – A security model emphasizing continuous authentication and least privilege access.

# 2. Books and Research Papers

- **"The Cybersecurity Handbook"** – A comprehensive guide covering security policies, risk management, and compliance strategies.

- **"Zero Trust Security: An Enterprise Guide"** – A detailed book on implementing Zero Trust frameworks in organizations.

- **"Cloud Security and Compliance"** – A resource focused on best practices for securing cloud environments and meeting regulatory requirements.

- **"AI and Cybersecurity"** – Research exploring the role of artificial intelligence in enhancing security operations and compliance monitoring.

- **"NIST Special Publications"** – Technical documents published by the National Institute of Standards and Technology, offering guidance on various cybersecurity topics.

# 3. Online Learning Platforms and Certifications

- **Certified Information Systems Security Professional (CISSP)** – A globally recognized certification for security professionals.

- **Certified Information Security Manager (CISM)** – Focuses on security governance, risk management, and compliance.

- **Certified Information Systems Auditor (CISA)** – A certification specializing in auditing, risk assessment, and information security controls.

- **Offensive Security Certified Professional (OSCP)** – A hands-on certification for penetration testing and ethical hacking.

- **Coursera, Udemy, and Cybrary** – Platforms offering cybersecurity courses, compliance training, and risk management programs.

# 4. Government and Industry Cybersecurity Portals

- **Cybersecurity and Infrastructure Security Agency (CISA)** – Government resources for cybersecurity guidelines, alerts, and risk management frameworks.

- **National Institute of Standards and Technology (NIST)** – Official security publications and compliance frameworks.

- **European Union Agency for Cybersecurity (ENISA)** – Guidance on cybersecurity policies, regulations, and best practices.

- **Center for Internet Security (CIS)** – Security benchmarks and best practices for system hardening.

These resources provide valuable knowledge for security professionals looking to enhance their expertise in cybersecurity governance, risk management, and compliance.

# Bibliography

[1] International Organization for Standardization, *ISO/IEC 27002: Code of Practice for Information Security Controls*, 2022. Available: `https://www.iso.org/standard/54533.html`

[2] National Institute of Standards and Technology (NIST), *Special Publication 1800: Cybersecurity Practice Guides*, 2021. Available: `https://www.nccoe.nist.gov/library`

[3] National Institute of Standards and Technology (NIST), *Cybersecurity for Internet of Things (IoT) Program*, 2021. Available: `https://www.nist.gov/programs-projects/cybersecurity-iot-program`

[4] MITRE Corporation, *MITRE ATT&CK Framework: Threat Intelligence and Adversary Tactics*, 2022. Available: `https://attack.mitre.org/`

[5] International Organization for Standardization, *ISO/IEC 22301: Business Continuity Management Systems*, 2019. Available: `https://www.iso.org/standard/75106.html`

[6] Center for Internet Security (CIS), *CIS Benchmarks for Secure System Configurations*, 2023. Available: `https://www.cisecurity.org/cis-benchmarks/`

[7] James Broad, *Red Teaming: The Art of Ethical Hacking*, Syngress, 2021.

[8] Georgia Weidman, *Penetration Testing: A Hands-On Introduction to Hacking*, No Starch Press, 2014.

[9] Eamon Dillon, *The Dark Web: The Cyber Underworld*, Merrion Press, 2021.

[10] David Kleidermacher and Mike Kleidermacher, *Embedded Systems Security: Practical Methods for Safe and Secure Software and Systems Development*, Elsevier, 2022.

[11] Christopher Hadnagy, *The Art of Human Hacking: Social Engineering Attacks and Defense*, Wiley, 2018.

[12] Allan Liska, *Ransomware: Defending Against Digital Extortion*, O'Reilly Media, 2021.

[13] James Scott, *The Hacking of America's Critical Infrastructure*, Institute for Critical Infrastructure Technology, 2017.

[14] Verizon, *Data Breach Investigations Report (DBIR)*, 2023. Available: `https://www.verizon.com/business/resources/reports/dbir/`

[15] IBM Security, *Cost of a Data Breach Report*, 2023. Available: `https://www.ibm.com/security/data-breach`

[16] Microsoft, *Microsoft Digital Defense Report*, 2023. Available: `https://www.microsoft.com/en-us/security/blog/microsoft-digital-defense-report/`

[17] FireEye Mandiant, *M-Trends Cyber Threat Intelligence Report*, 2023. Available: `https://www.mandiant.com/m-trends`

[18] European Union Agency for Cybersecurity (ENISA), *Threat Landscape Report*, 2023. Available: `https://www.enisa.europa.eu/publications`

[19] Gartner, *Top Cybersecurity Trends and Predictions*, 2023. Available: `https://www.gartner.com/en/insights/cybersecurity`

[20] EC-Council, *Certified Ethical Hacker (CEH) Training and Certification*, 2023. Available: `https://www.eccouncil.org/ceh/`

[21] Global Information Assurance Certification (GIAC), *GIAC Penetration Tester (GPEN) Certification*, 2023. Available: `https://www.giac.org/certification/penetration-tester-gpen/`

[22] SANS Institute, *Cybersecurity Training and Certification Programs*, 2023. Available: `https://www.sans.org/`

[23] International Organization for Standardization, *ISO/IEC 27001 Lead Auditor Certification*, 2023. Available: `https://www.iso.org/isoiec-27001-information-security.html`

# About the Author

**Pavan Paidy** is a thought leader and Information Security Consultant with over 13 years of experience in application security, cloud security, risk assessment, and compliance across finance, healthcare, and technology industries. He specializes in SAST, DAST, penetration testing, secure SDLC, and threat modeling, ensuring security at every development stage. Currently, he serves as a Security Lead at a leading cybersecurity company, contributing to security assessments, risk audits, and governance. Holding certifications such as CISA, CISM, CEH, along with an MBA in IT Business Management, he is an expert in cloud security and compliance. Passionate about cybersecurity, he mentors, conducts security awareness training, and collaborates on risk management strategies.